ORKNEY TRAVEL GUIDE

2024 Complete Companion To Explore The Seal Islands Like A Local With Everything You Need To Know, Things To Do & Maps

Gianna McMillon

Copyright

© Gianna McMillon, 2024.

All rights reserved.

No part of this publication may be reproduced, distributed, or transmitted in any form or by any means, including photocopying, recording, or other electronic or mechanical methods, without the prior written permission of the publisher, except in the case of brief quotations embodied in critical reviews and certain other noncommercial uses permitted by copyright law.

All images, graphics, and content within this guide are either owned by Gianna McMillon or used with permission from their respective owners. Any trademarks, service marks, product names, or named features are assumed to be the property of their respective owners and are used only for reference. There is no implied endorsement if we use one of these terms. Unauthorized use of any content in this publication may violate copyright, trademark, and other laws.

About The Author

Gianna McMillon is an avid traveler and seasoned travel guide author who has spent over two decades exploring the far corners of the world. Born with an insatiable curiosity and a love for adventure, Gianna has transformed her passion for travel into a successful writing career, inspiring countless readers to embark on their own journeys.

Gianna's travel guides are renowned for their meticulous detail, vivid descriptions, and practical advice, making them essential companions for travelers of all kinds. Her expertise spans diverse destinations, from the bustling streets of Tokyo and the romantic boulevards of Paris to the serene landscapes of New Zealand and the exotic locales of Southeast Asia.

With a background in cultural anthropology and a flair for storytelling, Gianna brings a unique perspective to her writing. She delves beyond the typical tourist attractions, uncovering hidden gems and local secrets that offer readers an authentic and immersive experience. Her guides not only provide logistical insights but also enrich the travel experience with historical context, cultural nuances, and personal anecdotes.

Gianna's work has been featured in prominent travel magazines and online platforms, earning her a loyal following of readers who eagerly anticipate her next adventure. When she's not exploring new destinations, Gianna enjoys sharing her experiences through engaging talks and workshops, inspiring others to see the world with fresh eyes.

Whether you're a seasoned traveler or a first-time explorer, Gianna McMillon's travel guides will equip you with the knowledge and inspiration to make your journey unforgettable.

TABLE OF CONTENTS

INTRODUCTION 8
   Welcome To Orkney 8
   Why Visit Orkney? 10
   How To Use This Guide 13
Chapter 2 17
EVERYTHING TO KNOW 17
   History And Culture 17
   Geography And Climate 22
   Language And Local Phrases 26
   Festivals And Events 31
Chapter 3 37
SPENDING WISELY 37
   Currency And Costs 37
   Budgeting Tips 42
   Money-Saving Hacks 47
   Best Value For Money Experiences 52
Chapter 4 58
MOVING AROUND 58
   Getting To Orkney 58
   Public Transportation 63
   Car Rentals And Driving Tips 68
   Cycling And Walking 73
   Ferry Services And Islands Hopping 78
Chapter 5 84
SLEEPING OVER 84

    Accommodation Options 84
    Hotels And Inns 84
    Bed And Breakfasts 90
    Hostels And Budget Stays 96
    Camping And Glamping 101
    Best Places To Stay 107
    Booking Tips And Advice 114

Chapter 6 120

EATING AND ADVENTURES 120

    Local Cuisine And Must-try Dishes 120
    Top Restaurants And Cafes 126
    Farmers Markets And Food Festivals 132
    Outdoor Adventures 135
    Hiking Trails 135
    Wildlife Watching 140
    Water Sports 146
    Historical And Archaeological Sites 152

Chapter 7 159

STAYING SAFE AND GREEN 159

    Safety Tips For Travelers 159
    Emergency Contacts And Sevices 164
    Eco-friendly Travel Practices 170
    Conservation And Responsible Tourism . 175

Chapter 8 181

ESSENTIAL PLANNING 181

    When To Visit 181
    Packing List 186
    Health And Travel Insurance 191

Visa And Entry Requirements 196
Chapter 9 .... **202**
SAMPLED ITINERARY **202**
Weekend Getaway 202
5-Day Adventure..................................... 207
7-Day Immersive Experience 213
Chapter 10 .... **221**
ICONIC LANDMARKS AND TOP TOURISM SPOTS **221**
Skara Brae 221
Ring Of Brodgar 225
Maeshowe 229
St. Magnus Cathedral............................ 234
The Old Man Of Hoy 240
Scapa Flow 242
Brough Of Birsay 245
Italian Chapel 248
CONCLUSION **251**
Final Tips And Recommendations 251
Staying Connected With Orkney 254

ORKNEY MAP

Scan Me

We Promise It Will Be Easy

How To Scan Code

1. Open a QR code scanning app or feature on your device.

2. Position the QR code within the frame of your device's camera.

3. Wait for the app or feature to recognize and scan the QR code.

4. Once scanned, the app or feature will usually display the information or take appropriate action.

5. If necessary, interact with the scanned content as desired.

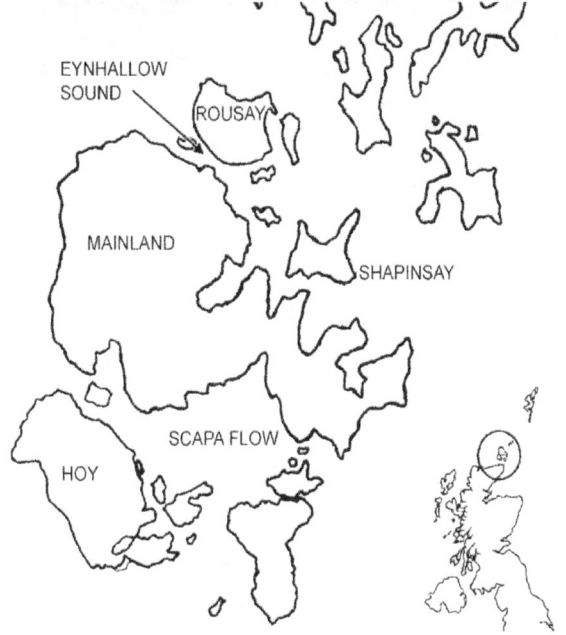

INTRODUCTION

Welcome To Orkney

Welcome to the Orkney Islands, a captivating archipelago where history, culture, and natural beauty converge. Located just off the northern coast of Scotland, Orkney is composed of about 70 islands, of which 20 are inhabited. This unique destination offers a rich tapestry of experiences, from ancient archaeological sites to stunning landscapes and a vibrant local community.

The Orkney Islands boast an extraordinary array of historical treasures, including some of the best-preserved Neolithic sites in Europe. Wander through ancient stone circles, burial mounds, and village ruins that date back over 5,000 years. These archaeological wonders, such as Skara Brae, the Ring of Brodgar, and Maeshowe, provide a fascinating glimpse into the lives of Orkney's early inhabitants.

Beyond its historical allure, Orkney is a paradise for nature enthusiasts. The islands are home to an abundance of wildlife, including puffins, seals, and orcas. The dramatic cliffs, pristine beaches, and rolling green hills offer endless opportunities for outdoor adventures, whether you're hiking, birdwatching, or simply soaking in the breathtaking scenery.

Orkney's vibrant culture is another compelling reason to visit. The islands are known for their strong sense of community and rich traditions, which are celebrated through various festivals and events throughout the year. From the spirited Orkney Folk Festival to the solemn St. Magnus Festival, these events showcase the islands' music, arts, and heritage, providing visitors with an immersive cultural experience.

In addition to its historical and natural attractions, Orkney offers modern comforts and amenities. You'll find a range of accommodations, from cozy bed and breakfasts to luxurious hotels, as well as a diverse culinary scene that highlights local produce and seafood. The friendly locals, known for their warmth and hospitality, are always ready to share their knowledge and stories, ensuring that your visit is both enjoyable and enriching.

Whether you're exploring the ancient ruins, admiring the stunning landscapes, or engaging with the local culture, Orkney promises a memorable and enriching experience. Welcome to Orkney, where every moment is a journey through time and a celebration of nature.

Why Visit Orkney?

Orkney offers an unparalleled journey through time, with its array of ancient sites that span over 5,000 years of history. These islands are home to some of the best-preserved Neolithic monuments in Europe, including the UNESCO World Heritage Site, the Heart of Neolithic Orkney. Explore the mystical stone circles of the Ring of Brodgar, the ancient village of Skara Brae, and the impressive tomb of Maeshowe, where Viking graffiti still adorns the walls. Each site offers a fascinating glimpse into the lives of the early inhabitants of these islands.

Stunning Natural Landscapes
Orkney's landscapes are as diverse as they are breathtaking. From dramatic sea cliffs and tranquil beaches to rolling hills and lush meadows, the islands offer a myriad of outdoor experiences. The

Old Man of Hoy, a towering sea stack, and the cliffs of Yesnaby are just a few examples of Orkney's striking coastal scenery. Whether you enjoy hiking, cycling, or simply soaking in the views, Orkney's natural beauty is sure to leave a lasting impression.

Rich Wildlife
Nature lovers will be thrilled by the abundant wildlife in Orkney. The islands are a haven for birdwatchers, with species such as puffins, gannets, and Arctic terns frequenting the area. The surrounding seas are home to seals, otters, and occasionally, orcas and dolphins. The islands' diverse habitats also support a range of flora, making it a wonderful destination for botanists and nature enthusiasts alike.

Vibrant Culture and Traditions
Orkney's culture is vibrant and deeply rooted in tradition. The islands host numerous festivals and events throughout the year, celebrating everything from folk music and storytelling to Viking heritage. The Orkney Folk Festival and the St. Magnus International Festival are highlights that attract visitors from around the world. These events provide an opportunity to experience the islands' music, arts, and community spirit firsthand.

Culinary Delights

Orkney's culinary scene is a treat for food lovers. The islands are known for their high-quality local produce, including Orkney beef, lamb, and seafood. Enjoy fresh scallops, crab, and lobster, or savor locally produced cheeses and whisky. Many restaurants and cafes emphasize farm-to-table dining, ensuring that visitors experience the best of Orkney's flavors.

Warm Hospitality
Orkney's residents are known for their warmth and hospitality. Whether you're staying in a cozy bed and breakfast or enjoying a pint in a local pub, you'll be welcomed with open arms. The islanders' friendly nature and willingness to share their knowledge and stories add a personal touch to your visit, making you feel right at home.

Adventure and Activities
For those seeking adventure, Orkney offers a range of activities. The islands are perfect for kayaking, sailing, and diving, with numerous shipwrecks and underwater sites to explore. Fishing, horse riding, and golf are also popular, providing plenty of options for an active holiday.

Unique Shopping Experience
Orkney's vibrant arts and crafts scene makes it a great destination for unique shopping. Local

artisans produce a range of handmade goods, including jewelry, pottery, textiles, and more. Visiting local shops and markets offers the chance to take home a piece of Orkney's creativity and craftsmanship.

In summary, Orkney is a destination that offers something for every traveler. Whether you're drawn by its rich history, stunning landscapes, diverse wildlife, vibrant culture, delicious food, or warm hospitality, the Orkney Islands promise a memorable and enriching experience. Come and discover the magic of Orkney for yourself.

How To Use This Guide

This guide is designed to help you plan and enjoy your visit to the Orkney Islands, offering comprehensive information on everything from historical sites and natural landscapes to practical travel tips and local culture. Here's how to make the most of this guide:

Navigating the Guide

The guide is divided into clear, easy-to-navigate sections, each focusing on a different aspect of your travel experience. Use the Table of Contents to quickly find the information you need, whether you're planning your itinerary, looking for accommodation, or searching for the best places to eat.

Comprehensive Information

Each section provides detailed information to help you plan your trip effectively. Whether you're interested in Orkney's history, outdoor activities, or cultural events, you'll find in-depth coverage to enhance your understanding and appreciation of the islands.

Practical Tips

Look for practical tips throughout the guide, highlighted in boxes or sidebars. These tips offer insider knowledge on topics such as budgeting, transportation, and safety, ensuring that you have a smooth and enjoyable trip.

Suggested Itineraries

The "Sampled Itineraries" section offers ready-made travel plans tailored to different lengths of stay and interests. Whether you're visiting for a weekend or a week, these itineraries provide a balanced mix of activities and must-see attractions, helping you make the most of your time in Orkney.

Local Insights

Throughout the guide, you'll find insights from local residents, providing a unique perspective on the best things to see and do. These insights offer valuable recommendations on hidden gems, local customs, and the best times to visit certain attractions.

Maps and Diagrams
Use the maps and diagrams provided in the "Appendices" section to familiarize yourself with the geography of Orkney. These visual aids help you navigate the islands, plan your routes, and locate key attractions and amenities.

Safety and Sustainability
Orkney is committed to sustainable tourism, and this guide emphasizes eco-friendly travel practices. In the "Staying Safe and Green" section, you'll find advice on how to minimize your environmental impact and travel responsibly. Additionally, safety tips are provided to ensure you have a secure and worry-free visit.

Personalizing Your Trip
The guide is designed to be flexible, allowing you to tailor your trip to your interests and preferences. Mix and match activities from different sections to create a personalized itinerary that suits your travel style, whether you're an adventure seeker, history enthusiast, or nature lover.

Keeping Updated

While this guide provides comprehensive information for 2024, it's always a good idea to check for the latest updates before your trip. Local events, weather conditions, and transportation schedules can change, so stay informed by visiting official tourism websites and local news sources.

Final Tips

Before you set off on your adventure, review the "Final Tips and Recommendations" in the Conclusion section. These last-minute pointers cover essential travel advice, ensuring that you're well-prepared for your journey.

By following this guide, you'll be well-equipped to explore the Orkney Islands and create unforgettable memories. Enjoy your trip and embrace the magic of Orkney!

Chapter 2

EVERYTHING TO KNOW

History And Culture

Journey Through Time

Prehistoric Beginnings

Orkney's history stretches back over 5,000 years, with evidence of human habitation dating to the Neolithic era. The islands are renowned for their exceptionally well-preserved archaeological sites. The Heart of Neolithic Orkney, a UNESCO World Heritage Site, includes the ancient village of Skara Brae, the ceremonial stone circles of the Ring of Brodgar and the Stones of Stenness, and the tomb of Maeshowe. These sites provide an extraordinary glimpse into prehistoric life, showcasing advanced construction techniques and a deep connection to the land and sky.

The Bronze and Iron Ages

The transition from the Neolithic to the Bronze Age saw the introduction of metalworking. Evidence of this period includes burial mounds, such as the impressive Unstan Chambered Cairn. The Iron Age brought further developments, including the construction of brochs—massive stone towers—such as the Broch of Gurness and Midhowe Broch. These structures reflect a society that was becoming more complex and defensive.

Norse Influence

In the 8th and 9th centuries, the Viking Age left an indelible mark on Orkney. Norse settlers established control over the islands, integrating them into the Norse Kingdom of Norway. This period saw the construction of important sites such as the Earls' Bu and Round Church in Orphir. The Orkneyinga Saga, a medieval manuscript, chronicles the lives and deeds of the Norse earls who ruled Orkney, providing a rich historical narrative of this era.

Medieval to Early Modern Period

In 1468, Orkney was pledged by Norway to Scotland as part of a dowry for the marriage of Margaret of Denmark to James III of Scotland. This transition marked the beginning of a new chapter in Orkney's history, characterized by the influence of Scottish and later British rule. The construction of St. Magnus Cathedral in Kirkwall during the 12th century stands as a testament to this period, blending Romanesque and Gothic architectural styles.

The Age of Exploration and Trade

The 16th to 18th centuries were marked by Orkney's strategic importance for maritime exploration and trade. The islands served as a vital stopover for ships traveling to the Arctic and North America. The Hudson's Bay Company recruited many Orcadians for their skills and resilience, significantly contributing to the fur trade in Canada. This period also saw agricultural advancements and the establishment of large estates.

Modern Era

The 20th century brought significant changes to Orkney, particularly during the World Wars. The strategic location of Scapa Flow, a large natural harbor, made it a key naval base. The sinking of the HMS Royal Oak by a German U-boat in 1939 is a poignant reminder of Orkney's wartime role. Postwar, Orkney continued to evolve, with developments in infrastructure, tourism, and renewable energy.

Cultural Richness

Language and Literature

Orkney's linguistic heritage is a blend of Old Norse and Scots, reflected in the distinctive Orcadian dialect. The islands have a rich literary tradition, with writers such as George Mackay Brown drawing inspiration from Orkney's landscapes and history. The Orkneyinga Saga remains a foundational text, offering a vivid account of the islands' Norse past.

Music and Festivals

Music plays a central role in Orkney's cultural life. The islands host several festivals, including the Orkney Folk Festival, which celebrates traditional and contemporary folk music, and the St. Magnus International Festival, which showcases a diverse range of artistic performances. These events highlight the islands' musical talent and cultural vibrancy.

Arts and Crafts

Orkney has a thriving arts and crafts scene, with local artisans producing everything from jewelry and pottery to textiles and paintings. Inspired by the natural beauty and heritage of the islands, these crafts are celebrated in local galleries and markets.

The Pier Arts Centre in Stromness is a notable venue that promotes contemporary visual art.

Folklore and Traditions
Orkney's folklore is rich with tales of mythical creatures, such as selkies (seal folk) and trows (trolls), reflecting the islands' deep connection to the sea and natural world. Traditional customs and celebrations, like the New Year's Ba' game in Kirkwall, continue to be an integral part of community life, blending historical roots with modern-day festivities.

Community and Heritage
The sense of community in Orkney is strong, with islanders maintaining a deep respect for their heritage. Local initiatives and heritage organizations work tirelessly to preserve Orkney's historical sites and traditions. This commitment to conservation ensures that the islands' rich history and culture are not only remembered but also celebrated and passed down to future generations.

Orkney's history and culture are a testament to the resilience and creativity of its people. From prehistoric times to the present day, the islands have been a crossroads of civilizations, each leaving its mark on the landscape and society. Today, Orkney continues to thrive, blending its ancient heritage with a vibrant contemporary culture, making it a truly unique and enriching destination.

Geography And Climate

Geography of Orkney

Location and Composition

The Orkney Islands are an archipelago located off the northern coast of Scotland, separated from the mainland by the Pentland Firth. The archipelago comprises around 70 islands, of which 20 are inhabited. The largest island, known as the "Mainland," serves as the central hub for transportation, commerce, and culture. Other notable islands include Hoy, Sanday, Stronsay, Rousay, and Westray.

Landscape and Topography

Orkney's landscape is characterized by its diverse and dramatic scenery. The Mainland features gentle rolling hills, fertile farmland, and extensive coastline with sandy beaches and rugged cliffs. The island of Hoy, in contrast, is more mountainous, with the highest peak, Ward Hill, rising to 481 meters (1,578 feet). Hoy is also home to the iconic Old Man of Hoy, a striking 137-meter (449-foot) sea stack popular with climbers.

The coastline of Orkney is varied, with sheltered bays, dramatic cliffs, and rocky shores. The beaches, such as those at Skaill Bay and Waulkmill Bay, are known for their pristine sands and crystal-clear waters. The sea around Orkney is rich in marine life and provides opportunities for fishing, diving, and wildlife watching.

Geology
Orkney's geological history is as fascinating as its human history. The islands are primarily composed of Old Red Sandstone, formed around 400 million years ago during the Devonian period. This sedimentary rock creates the distinctive cliffs and formations seen across the islands. The flagstones and sandstones are often layered and can contain fossils, providing a window into ancient ecosystems.

The glacial activity during the last Ice Age also shaped Orkney's landscape, leaving behind features such as glacial valleys, moraines, and lochs. The islands' geology is integral to understanding the archaeological sites, as many ancient structures were built using local stone.

Climate of Orkney

General Climate

Orkney experiences a maritime climate, influenced by its northern location and surrounding seas. The climate is characterized by cool summers, mild winters, and relatively high humidity. The North Atlantic Drift, a branch of the Gulf Stream, helps moderate temperatures, preventing extreme cold despite Orkney's latitude.

Seasonal Variations
- Spring (March to May): Spring in Orkney is marked by gradually warming temperatures and increasing daylight. Average temperatures range from 5°C (41°F) to 10°C (50°F). This season sees the blooming of wildflowers and the return of migratory birds, making it an ideal time for nature enthusiasts.

- Summer (June to August): Summer brings the longest days of the year, with up to 18 hours of daylight in June. Temperatures range from 10°C (50°F) to 15°C (59°F), occasionally reaching 20°C (68°F) on warm days. The extended daylight hours allow for long days of exploration and outdoor activities.

- Autumn (September to November): Autumn sees a gradual cooling of temperatures, ranging from 6°C (43°F) to 12°C (54°F). The landscape takes on rich autumnal hues, and the skies often display stunning sunsets. This season also marks the beginning of the migratory bird departure.

- Winter (December to February): Winter is mild but can be windy and wet. Temperatures generally range from 2°C (36°F) to 7°C (45°F). The shortest days occur in December, with only around six hours of daylight. Despite the shorter days, winter is a time of rich cultural activity, with various festivals and events.

Wind and Precipitation

Orkney is known for its windy conditions, with strong gales especially common in winter. The prevailing winds come from the southwest, but the islands can experience winds from all directions. Wind speeds can reach over 100 km/h (62 mph) during storms, influencing both daily life and the landscape.

Precipitation is evenly distributed throughout the year, with an average annual rainfall of about 1,000 mm (39 inches). Rainfall can vary significantly across the islands, with the western parts generally receiving more rain than the eastern areas. Despite frequent rain, Orkney also enjoys clear and bright days, particularly in the summer.

Light and Daylight

The amount of daylight varies dramatically throughout the year due to Orkney's high latitude. In midsummer, the islands experience "Simmer Dim," where twilight extends throughout the night, providing nearly continuous daylight. Conversely, in midwinter, daylight is limited, with long nights and short days. These variations in light influence daily activities and seasonal events.

Orkney's geography and climate are integral to its identity, shaping the natural environment, wildlife, and human activities. The islands' diverse landscapes, from fertile farmlands to rugged cliffs, combined with a maritime climate, create a unique setting that is both beautiful and challenging. Whether you're exploring the geological wonders, enjoying the long summer days, or braving the winter winds, Orkney's geography and climate offer a distinctive and enriching experience.

Language And Local Phrases

The Orkney Islands have a rich linguistic history influenced by several languages over the centuries. Originally inhabited by the Picts, the language spoken would have been a form of Pictish, about which little is known. With the arrival of the Norse settlers in the 8th and 9th centuries, Old Norse became the dominant language. This influence persisted for many centuries, and even today, traces of Old Norse can be found in the local dialect and place names.

In the 15th century, when Orkney became part of Scotland, Scots began to replace Norse as the primary language. Over time, a unique blend of Scots and Norse evolved, resulting in the distinctive Orcadian dialect spoken today.

The Orcadian Dialect
The Orcadian dialect is a variety of Scots that incorporates many Norse words and phrases. It has a distinct pronunciation and vocabulary that can be unfamiliar to visitors. While English is universally spoken and understood, the local dialect adds a layer of cultural richness to the Orkney experience.

Orcadian pronunciation tends to be softer than mainland Scots, with a musical lilt that reflects the islands' Norse heritage. Certain consonant sounds may be pronounced differently, and there are unique vowel sounds not found in standard English.

Local Phrases and Expressions
To help you immerse yourself in the local culture and communicate more effectively with the islanders, here are some common Orcadian phrases and expressions:

Greetings and Polite Expressions
- Hello: "Hallo" or "Hid hidder"
- Goodbye: "Fare-ye-weel"
- Thank you: "Thankee"
- Please: "Please" (similar to standard English)
- Yes: "Aye"
- No: "Naw"

Everyday Conversation
- How are you? "Hou's thee?" or "Hoo's things wi' thee?"
- I'm fine, thank you. "I'm fine, thankee."
- What's your name? "Whit's dy name?"
- My name is... "Me name is..."
- Where are you from? "Whaur bides thee?"
- I'm from... "I'm fae..."

Common Phrases
- It's a fine day. "Hit's a braw day."
- The weather is good. "Da weather's fine."
- How much is this? "Hou muckle is dis?"
- That's expensive. "Dat's dear."
- That's cheap. "Dat's chape."

Directions and Travel
- Where is the bus stop? "Whaur's da bus stop?"
- How do I get to... ? "Hou dae I get tae... ?"
- Turn left/right. "Turn left/right."

- Straight ahead. "Stairt aheid."

Food and Drink
- What's for dinner? "Whit's for denner?"
- Can I have a cup of tea? "Kin I hae a cuppa tea?"
- This is delicious. "Dis is delish."
- I'm hungry/thirsty. "I'm hunger't/thirsty."

Local Terminology
- House: "Hoose"
- Child: "Bairn"
- Man: "Man"
- Woman: "Wifie"
- Friend: "Freend"
- Yes: "Aye"
- No: "Naw"
- Very: "Real" (e.g., "real cold" means "very cold")
- Now: "Noo"

Understanding Local Names
Orkney place names often have Norse origins, reflecting the islands' Viking past. Understanding these can enhance your visit and help you navigate the islands. Here are some common elements in Orkney place names:

- bister: From Old Norse "býstaðr," meaning farm or homestead (e.g., Orphir).

- breck: From Old Norse "brekka," meaning slope or hillside (e.g., Birsay).
- holm: From Old Norse "holmr," meaning small island or islet (e.g., Holm).
- wick: From Old Norse "vík," meaning bay or inlet (e.g., Kirkwall, meaning "Church Bay").

While English is widely spoken in Orkney, taking the time to learn and use some local phrases and understand the dialect can greatly enrich your travel experience. The Orcadian dialect is a testament to the islands' unique cultural heritage, blending influences from Norse and Scots. By embracing the local language, you'll not only connect more deeply with the people of Orkney but also gain a greater appreciation for the islands' rich history and vibrant culture.

Festivals And Events

The Orkney Islands are renowned for their lively and diverse cultural scene, which is celebrated through numerous festivals and events throughout the year. These gatherings offer visitors a unique opportunity to experience the islands' rich heritage, vibrant arts, and strong community spirit. From traditional music and dance to contemporary arts and Viking re-enactments, Orkney's festivals are a testament to the islands' dynamic culture.

Major Festivals and Events
Orkney Folk Festival
- When: Late May
- Where: Various locations, primarily Stromness
- Description: The Orkney Folk Festival is one of the most anticipated events in the islands' cultural calendar. It brings together local and international folk musicians for a four-day celebration of music,

song, and dance. With performances in venues ranging from cozy pubs to large halls, the festival offers an intimate and authentic folk music experience. Workshops, ceilidhs (traditional dances), and informal sessions add to the festival's vibrant atmosphere.

St. Magnus International Festival
- When: Late June
- Where: Kirkwall and other locations
- Description: Named after Orkney's patron saint, St. Magnus, this prestigious arts festival showcases a diverse range of performances, including classical music, theater, dance, literature, and visual arts. The festival attracts world-class artists and performers, making it a highlight for culture enthusiasts. Events take place in various venues, including the stunning St. Magnus Cathedral, providing a magnificent backdrop for many performances.

Orkney International Science Festival
- When: Early September
- Where: Various locations, primarily Kirkwall
- Description: The Orkney International Science Festival is a week-long event that explores the wonders of science and its connections to the islands' environment, history, and culture. The festival features lectures, workshops, exhibitions, and interactive activities for all ages. Topics range

from archaeology and astronomy to renewable energy and marine biology, reflecting Orkney's unique scientific and natural heritage.

The Ba' Game
- When: Christmas Day and New Year's Day
- Where: Kirkwall
- Description: The Ba' Game is a traditional Orkney sport with deep historical roots. Played in the streets of Kirkwall, the game involves two teams—the Uppies and the Doonies—battling to carry a leather ball to their respective goals. The game is a thrilling and chaotic spectacle, drawing large crowds of participants and spectators. The Ba' Game is a unique expression of Orkney's community spirit and competitive zeal.

Orkney Blues Festival
- When: Mid-September
- Where: Various locations, primarily Stromness
- Description: The Orkney Blues Festival brings together blues musicians from Orkney, the UK, and beyond for a weekend of soulful music. Performances take place in pubs, hotels, and outdoor venues, creating a relaxed and friendly atmosphere. The festival includes jam sessions, workshops, and open mic nights, offering both seasoned musicians and newcomers a chance to showcase their talents.

Orkney Storytelling Festival
- When: Late October
- Where: Various locations
- Description: The Orkney Storytelling Festival celebrates the islands' rich oral traditions through a series of storytelling sessions, performances, and workshops. The festival features local and visiting storytellers who share myths, legends, folktales, and personal stories. Events take place in intimate settings such as community halls and historic sites, allowing for a deeply immersive experience.

Seasonal and Community Events
Lambing Season
- When: April to May
- Where: Various farms
- Description: While not a festival in the traditional sense, lambing season is a special time in Orkney. Visitors can witness the birth of lambs and learn about sheep farming, which is an integral part of the islands' agricultural heritage. Many farms open their doors to visitors, offering tours and hands-on experiences.

Orkney Nature Festival
- When: May
- Where: Various locations

- Description: The Orkney Nature Festival celebrates the islands' stunning natural environment and diverse wildlife. The festival features guided walks, boat trips, wildlife watching, and educational workshops. Participants can explore Orkney's rich biodiversity, from seabird colonies and marine mammals to wildflowers and coastal landscapes.

Agricultural Shows
- When: Various dates in summer
- Where: Various locations, including Dounby, East Mainland, and County Show in Kirkwall
- Description: Orkney's agricultural shows are vibrant community events that highlight the islands' farming traditions. These shows feature livestock competitions, craft displays, food stalls, and entertainment for all ages. They provide a glimpse into rural life and the importance of agriculture to Orkney's economy and culture.

Christmas and New Year Celebrations
- When: December to January
- Where: Various locations
- Description: The festive season in Orkney is marked by a series of community events, markets, and celebrations. Kirkwall's Winter Festival includes a Christmas market, light displays, and festive performances. The New Year is welcomed

with traditional customs, including the Hogmanay celebrations and the New Year's Day Ba' Game.

Orkney's festivals and events offer a window into the islands' rich cultural heritage and vibrant community life. Whether you're a music lover, art enthusiast, science buff, or simply looking to experience local traditions, there's something for everyone. These celebrations not only provide entertainment and enjoyment but also foster a sense of connection to Orkney's unique identity and history. Make sure to check the event calendars and plan your visit around these exciting festivals to fully immerse yourself in the spirit of Orkney.

Chapter 3

SPENDING WISELY

Currency And Costs

The currency used in Orkney, like the rest of Scotland, is the British Pound Sterling (£), abbreviated as GBP. Banknotes and coins are issued in various denominations:
- Banknotes: £5, £10, £20, £50
- Coins: 1p, 2p, 5p, 10p, 20p, 50p, £1, £2

Scottish banks issue their own banknotes, which are legal tender throughout the UK. However, some places outside Scotland may be unfamiliar with them, so it's advisable to carry a mix of Scottish and English banknotes.

Currency Exchange
Currency exchange services are available at major banks in Kirkwall and Stromness, as well as at the Kirkwall Airport. ATMs are widespread in these areas, and they usually offer competitive exchange rates. It's a good idea to exchange some money before arriving if you plan to travel to more remote islands, where banking facilities might be limited.

Costs in Orkney

Accommodation
- Budget: Hostels and campsites offer the most affordable options, ranging from £15 to £30 per night.
- Mid-Range: Guesthouses, B&Bs, and mid-range hotels typically cost between £60 and £120 per night.
- Luxury: High-end hotels and self-catering cottages can range from £150 to £250 per night, depending on the season and amenities.

Dining and Food
- Budget: Casual cafes, bakeries, and takeaway shops offer meals for around £5 to £10.
- Mid-Range: Pub meals and mid-range restaurants typically cost between £10 and £20 per person for a main course.

- High-End: Fine dining establishments and seafood restaurants can range from £25 to £50 per person for a full meal.

Transportation
- Public Transport: Bus fares are affordable, usually ranging from £1 to £5 for local routes. Day passes and multi-day passes offer cost savings for frequent travelers.
- Car Rental: Renting a car can cost between £30 and £60 per day, depending on the vehicle type and rental company. Fuel prices are similar to mainland Scotland, averaging around £1.30 to £1.50 per liter.
- Ferries: Inter-island ferry fares vary depending on the distance. For example, a return trip from Kirkwall to Westray costs around £20 for an adult passenger and £60 for a car.

Attractions and Activities
- Historical Sites: Entry fees to popular attractions such as Skara Brae, Maeshowe, and the Italian Chapel range from £5 to £15. Many outdoor sites, such as the Ring of Brodgar and the Old Man of Hoy, are free to visit.
- Tours and Excursions: Guided tours, wildlife excursions, and boat trips typically cost between £30 and £100 per person, depending on the length and type of tour.

- Events and Festivals: Ticket prices for festivals and events vary widely. For example, a concert at the Orkney Folk Festival might cost around £15, while entry to the St. Magnus International Festival performances can range from £10 to £30.

Tips for Spending Wisely

<u>Plan Ahead</u>
- Advance Bookings: Book accommodation and transportation in advance to secure the best rates, especially during peak tourist season (June to August) and major festivals.
- Off-Peak Travel: Consider visiting during the shoulder seasons (spring and autumn) when prices for accommodation and activities may be lower, and the islands are less crowded.

<u>Budget Accommodation and Dining</u>
- Self-Catering: Opt for self-catering accommodations, such as cottages or apartments, which allow you to prepare your own meals and save on dining costs.
- Local Produce: Shop at local markets and stores for fresh, affordable ingredients to cook your meals. Orkney is known for its high-quality local produce, including seafood, cheese, and meats.

<u>Transportation Savings</u>

- Public Transport: Use public buses and ferries to explore the islands. Multi-day passes and group tickets can offer significant savings.
- Bike Rentals: Consider renting a bicycle for an eco-friendly and cost-effective way to get around, especially on the smaller islands.

Free and Low-Cost Activities
- Outdoor Exploration: Take advantage of Orkney's stunning natural landscapes, which offer numerous opportunities for hiking, birdwatching, and photography at no cost.
- Local Museums: Visit local museums and heritage centers, many of which have free entry or accept donations.

Currency Exchange and Payment Methods
- ATM Withdrawals: Use ATMs to withdraw cash in small amounts as needed to avoid carrying large sums. Be mindful of potential foreign transaction fees if using a non-UK bank card.
- Card Payments: Credit and debit cards are widely accepted in Orkney, including in smaller shops and cafes. However, it's always useful to have some cash on hand for small purchases or in more remote areas.

Visiting Orkney can be a memorable and enriching experience without breaking the bank. By planning ahead, taking advantage of budget-friendly options, and spending wisely, you can enjoy all that these beautiful islands have to offer. From exploring historical sites and enjoying local cuisine to participating in festivals and outdoor activities, Orkney provides a wealth of experiences that cater to a variety of budgets.

Budgeting Tips

Planning Your Budget

Visiting Orkney can be an enriching experience without straining your finances. Careful planning and smart spending can help you make the most of your trip. Here are some practical budgeting tips to ensure you have a memorable and affordable visit to the Orkney Islands.

Accommodation

Book Early

- Advance Reservations: Especially during peak tourist season (June to August) and major festivals, booking your accommodation well in advance can secure the best rates and availability.
- Off-Peak Travel: Consider visiting during the shoulder seasons (spring and autumn) when prices for accommodation are generally lower.

Budget-Friendly Options

- Hostels and Campsites: These offer the most affordable lodging, ranging from £15 to £30 per night.
- B&Bs and Guesthouses: Mid-range options usually cost between £60 and £120 per night and often include breakfast.
- Self-Catering: Renting a cottage or apartment allows you to cook your meals, saving money on dining out.

Dining and Food

Eat Like a Local
- Local Markets: Shop for fresh produce at local markets and stores. Orkney is known for its high-quality local produce, including seafood, cheese, and meats.
- Self-Catering: If you're staying in self-catering accommodation, cooking your own meals can significantly reduce food expenses.

Budget Dining
- Cafes and Bakeries: Casual eateries offer meals for around £5 to £10.
- Pub Meals: Enjoy hearty and affordable meals in local pubs, with main courses typically costing between £10 and £20.
- Takeaways: Fish and chips, sandwiches, and other takeout options are both tasty and economical.

Transportation

Public Transport
- Bus Services: Use Orkney's efficient bus system to travel between towns and attractions. A day pass can offer unlimited travel for a fixed price, usually between £5 and £10.
- Ferry Services: For island hopping, ferries are essential. Check for multi-trip discounts or passes to save on travel costs.

Car Rentals and Alternatives
- Car Rentals: If you prefer the convenience of a car, compare rental rates and book in advance. Prices range from £30 to £60 per day.
- Biking: Renting a bicycle is an eco-friendly and cost-effective way to explore the islands, especially on the smaller ones.

Activities and Attractions

Free and Low-Cost Attractions
- Historical Sites: Many outdoor sites, such as the Ring of Brodgar and the Old Man of Hoy, are free to visit. For paid sites, look for combination tickets or discounts.
- Museums: Visit local museums and heritage centers, many of which have free entry or accept donations.

- Nature Activities: Take advantage of Orkney's natural beauty with activities like hiking, birdwatching, and beachcombing.

Festivals and Events
- Local Festivals: Many festivals and events offer free or low-cost entry. Check the schedule and plan to attend these cultural celebrations.
- Workshops and Tours: Participate in affordable workshops or guided tours to enhance your experience without overspending.

Money Management

Currency Exchange
- ATMs: Use ATMs to withdraw cash as needed to avoid carrying large amounts. Be mindful of potential fees if using a non-UK bank card.
- Exchange Rates: Check exchange rates and fees when converting money. Airports and banks typically offer better rates than hotels or currency exchange booths.

Payment Methods
- Credit and Debit Cards: Widely accepted throughout Orkney, including in smaller shops and cafes. However, always carry some cash for small purchases or in remote areas where card facilities might not be available.

Additional Tips

Discounts and Passes
- Visitor Passes: Look for visitor passes that offer discounts on multiple attractions or services. These can provide significant savings if you plan to visit several sites.
- Student and Senior Discounts: Always ask about available discounts if you are a student, senior, or part of another eligible group.

Local Insights
- Ask Locals: Residents often know the best and most affordable places to eat, shop, and visit. Don't hesitate to ask for recommendations.
- Community Boards: Check local community boards and websites for information on events, deals, and discounts.

Flexible Itinerary
- Adapt Plans: Be flexible with your itinerary to take advantage of last-minute deals or unexpected opportunities for savings.

By planning carefully and using these budgeting tips, you can enjoy a rich and fulfilling experience in Orkney without overspending. From selecting cost-effective accommodations and dining options to making the most of public transportation and free attractions, there are many ways to spend wisely while soaking in the unique charm and culture of the Orkney Islands. Whether you're a budget traveler or simply looking to maximize your travel value, these strategies will help you make the most of your trip.

Money-Saving Hacks

Visiting the Orkney Islands can be a rewarding experience without straining your budget. Here are some effective money-saving hacks to help you explore Orkney while keeping your expenses in check.

Accommodation Hacks

Stay in Hostels or Campsites
- Affordable Lodging: Opt for hostels or campsites, which are the most budget-friendly options, costing between £15 and £30 per night.
- Social Experience: Hostels offer the added benefit of meeting fellow travelers, potentially sharing tips and travel stories.

Book in Advance
- Early Reservations: Booking your accommodation well in advance, especially during peak seasons, can secure better rates and availability.

- Off-Peak Travel: Consider visiting during the shoulder seasons (spring and autumn) when accommodation prices are generally lower.

Self-Catering Options
- Save on Meals: Renting a self-catering cottage or apartment allows you to cook your own meals, which can significantly reduce dining costs.
- Local Ingredients: Purchase fresh, local produce from markets and stores to prepare your meals.

Dining and Food Hacks

Eat Like a Local
- Local Markets: Shop for fresh produce, seafood, cheese, and meats at local markets, which are often more affordable than restaurants.
- Home-Cooked Meals: Cooking your own meals in self-catering accommodations can save a lot on dining expenses.

Budget Dining
- Cafes and Bakeries: Casual eateries, cafes, and bakeries offer affordable meals, typically ranging from £5 to £10.
- Pubs and Takeaways: Enjoy hearty and budget-friendly meals at local pubs and takeaways, with main courses costing between £10 and £20.

Transportation Hacks

Use Public Transport
- Bus Services: Orkney's efficient bus system is an affordable way to travel between towns and attractions. Day passes offer unlimited travel for a fixed price, usually between £5 and £10.
- Multi-Trip Passes: Look for multi-trip discounts or passes for inter-island ferries to save on travel costs.

Rent Bicycles
- Eco-Friendly Option: Renting a bicycle is a cost-effective and environmentally friendly way to explore the islands, especially the smaller ones.
- Health Benefits: Biking is not only economical but also a great way to stay active during your trip.

Car Sharing
- Travel Together: If you're renting a car, consider sharing the cost with fellow travelers. This can significantly reduce transportation expenses and make exploring more social and fun.

Activity and Attraction Hacks
Free and Low-Cost Attractions
- Historical Sites: Many outdoor sites, such as the Ring of Brodgar and the Old Man of Hoy, are free to visit.
- Museums: Visit local museums and heritage centers, many of which have free entry or accept donations.

Participate in Local Events
- Community Events: Many local festivals and community events offer free or low-cost entry. Check local listings for upcoming events during your visit.
- Workshops and Tours: Look for affordable workshops and guided tours to enhance your experience without overspending.

General Money-Saving Hacks

Currency Exchange
- Use ATMs: Withdraw cash from ATMs as needed to avoid carrying large amounts. Be mindful of potential fees if using a non-UK bank card.
- Compare Rates: Check exchange rates and fees when converting money. Airports and banks typically offer better rates than hotels or currency exchange booths.

Use Credit and Debit Cards
- Widely Accepted: Credit and debit cards are widely accepted throughout Orkney, including in smaller shops and cafes. However, always carry some cash for small purchases or in remote areas where card facilities might not be available.

Look for Discounts and Passes

- Visitor Passes: Consider purchasing visitor passes that offer discounts on multiple attractions or services.
- Student and Senior Discounts: Always ask about available discounts if you are a student, senior, or part of another eligible group.

Plan and Adapt
- Flexible Itinerary: Be flexible with your plans to take advantage of last-minute deals or unexpected opportunities for savings.
- Local Recommendations: Ask locals for their recommendations on affordable dining, shopping, and attractions.

Specific Tips for Orkney

Ferry Deals
- Return Tickets: When traveling between islands, purchase return tickets instead of one-way to save on ferry costs.
- Group Discounts: If traveling with family or friends, inquire about group discounts for ferries and other transportation options.

Free Guided Walks
- Local Guides: Some local guides offer free or donation-based walking tours, providing insightful information about the area without a high cost.

Pack Snacks and Drinks
- Picnic Supplies: Bring snacks and drinks for day trips to avoid buying expensive items at tourist sites.
- Reusable Water Bottle: Carry a reusable water bottle to refill throughout the day, saving money and reducing plastic waste.

Exploring Orkney on a budget is entirely possible with a little planning and smart spending. By following these money-saving hacks, you can enjoy all the rich cultural heritage, stunning landscapes, and unique experiences the islands have to offer without breaking the bank. Whether it's choosing budget-friendly accommodation, cooking your own meals, or taking advantage of free attractions, these tips will help you make the most of your visit to Orkney.

Best Value For Money Experiences

Orkney offers a wealth of experiences that provide excellent value for money, allowing visitors to enjoy the islands' rich history, stunning landscapes, and vibrant culture without breaking the bank. Here are some of the best value-for-money experiences you can enjoy in Orkney.

Exploring Historical Sites

Skara Brae
- Description: One of the best-preserved Neolithic settlements in Europe, Skara Brae offers a fascinating glimpse into ancient life.
- Cost: Entry fee is around £9 for adults, with discounts available for children, seniors, and families.
- Value: The site includes a visitor center with informative exhibits and a reconstructed house, providing excellent educational value.

Ring of Brodgar
- Description: This impressive stone circle and henge, dating back to the late Neolithic period, is a must-visit.
- Cost: Free entry.
- Value: The site offers stunning views and a sense of ancient history, all at no cost.

Maeshowe
- Description: A large Neolithic chambered cairn, famous for its winter solstice alignment and Viking runes.
- Cost: Entry fee is around £7 for adults, with discounts for children and seniors.
- Value: Guided tours provide in-depth historical context and insights into this ancient tomb.

Natural Wonders

Old Man of Hoy
- Description: A striking 137-meter sea stack on the west coast of Hoy, popular with hikers and climbers.
- Cost: Free to visit.
- Value: The dramatic coastal scenery and challenging hike make this a rewarding experience for nature lovers.

Orkney Mainland Coastal Walks
- Description: Numerous coastal trails offer breathtaking views, wildlife watching, and opportunities for photography.
- Cost: Free.
- Value: Enjoy Orkney's stunning natural beauty and diverse wildlife without any expense.

Marwick Head RSPB Reserve
- Description: A cliff-top nature reserve home to thousands of seabirds, including puffins, razorbills, and kittiwakes.
- Cost: Free entry.
- Value: Ideal for birdwatching and enjoying the rugged coastal landscape.

Cultural Experiences

Orkney Museums
- Orkney Museum (Kirkwall): Explore Orkney's history from the Stone Age to the present day.

- Cost: Free entry.
- Value: Comprehensive exhibits and artifacts provide deep insights into Orkney's heritage.

- Stromness Museum: Features maritime history, natural history, and local artifacts.
- Cost: Modest entry fee, usually around £5.
- Value: A rich collection of exhibits for a small fee.

Local Festivals
- Orkney Folk Festival (May): Experience traditional and contemporary folk music from local and international artists.
- Cost: Tickets for individual events are reasonably priced, with some free sessions.
- Value: High-quality music performances and community atmosphere.

- St. Magnus International Festival (June): A diverse arts festival featuring music, theater, dance, and literature.
- Cost: Varied ticket prices, with some free events.
- Value: World-class performances in unique venues like St. Magnus Cathedral.

Affordable Activities
Beachcombing and Wildlife Watching

- Description: Orkney's beaches are perfect for collecting shells, spotting seals, and observing seabirds.
- Cost: Free.
-Value: Enjoy hours of exploration and discovery along the coastliuided Walks and Tours
- Local Guides: Some local guides offer free or donation-based walking tours.
- Value: Gain valuable insights and stories from knowledgeable guides at little to no cost.

Dining on a Budget

Local Cafes and Pubs
- Cafes: Enjoy hearty soups, sandwiches, and baked goods at local cafes for around £5 to £10.
- Pubs: Many pubs offer affordable and filling meals, with main courses typically costing between £10 and £20.
- Value: Delicious local cuisine and a chance to experience Orkney's hospitality.

Farmers' Markets
- Description: Purchase fresh, local produce and handmade goods directly from farmers and artisans.
- Cost: Prices vary but are generally affordable.
- Value: High-quality, locally-sourced food and crafts provide great value and support the local economy.

Tips for Maximizing Value
- Multi-Site Tickets: Look for combination tickets or passes that offer entry to multiple historical sites at a discounted rate.
- Discounts: Always inquire about available discounts for students, seniors, families, and groups.
- Off-Peak Visits: Visit popular attractions during off-peak times to avoid crowds and potentially lower costs.

Orkney offers a variety of experiences that provide excellent value for money, from exploring ancient historical sites and stunning natural landscapes to enjoying cultural festivals and local cuisine. By taking advantage of free and low-cost activities, affordable dining options, and strategic planning, you can enjoy a rich and fulfilling visit to the Orkney Islands without overspending. Whether you're a history buff, nature enthusiast, or culture lover, Orkney has something to offer every traveler on a budget.

Chapter 4

MOVING AROUND

Getting To Orkney

Reaching the Orkney Islands involves a journey across sea or air, with various transportation options to suit different preferences and budgets. This guide will help you navigate the best ways to get to Orkney, ensuring a smooth start to your adventure.

By Air

Direct Flights
- Airlines: Loganair operates direct flights to Kirkwall Airport (KOI) from several UK airports.
- Departure Cities: Flights are available from Aberdeen, Edinburgh, Glasgow, and Inverness.

- Flight Duration: Typically 1-2 hours, depending on the departure city.
- Cost: Prices vary, but booking in advance can secure flights for around £60-£150 one way.
- Airport Facilities: Kirkwall Airport offers basic amenities including a cafe, car rental services, and taxi stands.

By Sea

Ferry Services
- Operators: NorthLink Ferries and Pentland Ferries are the main operators providing services to Orkney.
- Routes:
    - NorthLink Ferries: From Aberdeen to Kirkwall (via Lerwick) and from Scrabster to Stromness.
    - Pentland Ferries: From Gills Bay (near John O'Groats) to St. Margaret's Hope on South Ronaldsay.
- Travel Time:
    - Aberdeen to Kirkwall: Approximately 6 hours.
    - Scrabster to Stromness: About 90 minutes.
    - Gills Bay to St. Margaret's Hope: Around 1 hour.
- Cost: Fares vary depending on the route, season, and whether you're traveling with a vehicle. Prices range from £20-£30 for foot passengers and £50-£150 for vehicles.

- Booking Tips: Book ferries well in advance, especially during peak seasons, to secure the best rates and availability.

By Land and Sea
Driving to Ferry Ports
- From Inverness to Scrabster: Approximately 2.5 hours by car. The scenic drive takes you through the Scottish Highlands.
- From Inverness to Gills Bay: Around 3 hours by car. Another picturesque route offering stunning landscapes.
- Parking: Secure long-term parking options are available at ferry ports.

Public Transport
Train and Bus Services
- Train to Thurso: Take a train from Inverness to Thurso, then a short bus or taxi ride to Scrabster for the ferry to Stromness.
- Train to Wick: Alternatively, take a train from Inverness to Wick, then a bus or taxi to Gills Bay for the Pentland Ferries service.
- Cost: Train fares vary, with advance tickets offering significant savings. Expect to pay around £20-£50 one way.
- Travel Time: The train journey from Inverness to Thurso or Wick takes approximately 4 hours.

Combination Tickets
Travel Packages
- NorthLink Ferries: Offers combined train and ferry tickets for seamless travel. These packages often include discounts and can simplify your journey planning.
- Rail and Sail: ScotRail's Rail and Sail tickets combine train travel with ferry services to Orkney, providing a cost-effective and convenient option.

Getting Around Orkney
Car Rentals
- Availability: Car rentals are available at Kirkwall Airport and in Kirkwall town center.
- Cost: Rates range from £30-£60 per day, depending on the vehicle type and rental duration.
- Booking Book in advance to ensure availability, especially during peak tourist season.

Public Transport
- Bus Services: Orkney has a reliable bus network connecting major towns and attractions. Day passes offer unlimited travel for a fixed price, typically between £5 and £10.
- Ferry Services: Inter-island ferries operated by Orkney Ferries connect the mainland with outlying islands. Multi-trip passes can save money if you plan to visit several islands.

Tips for a Smooth Journey

Plan Ahead
- Advance Bookings: Whether flying or taking the ferry, booking tickets in advance can secure the best rates and ensure availability.
- Check Schedules: Ferry and flight schedules can vary seasonally, so confirm times close to your travel date.

Pack Appropriately
- Travel Essentials: Pack layers and waterproof clothing, as weather can change quickly. Bring essentials like travel documents, snacks, and entertainment for the journey.
- Luggage: Be mindful of luggage restrictions on flights and ferries. Consider packing light to make your journey more convenient.

Stay Informed
- Weather Updates: Monitor weather forecasts, especially if traveling by ferry, as services can be affected by adverse conditions.
- Travel Alerts Stay informed about any travel alerts or disruptions that might impact your journey.

Getting to Orkney is an integral part of the adventure, offering opportunities to enjoy scenic landscapes and coastal views. Whether you choose to fly or take a ferry, planning ahead and considering your options will ensure a smooth and enjoyable start to your Orkney experience. By following these tips and making use of the various transportation options available, you can look forward to a memorable and hassle-free journey to the Orkney Islands.

Public Transportation

Orkney boasts an efficient and reliable public transportation system, making it easy to explore the islands without the need for a private vehicle. Here's a comprehensive guide to getting around Orkney using public transportation.

Bus Services

Main Bus Operator
- Stagecoach Orkney: The primary bus service provider on the Orkney Mainland and some of the connected islands. The buses are modern and comfortable, offering a convenient way to travel between towns and attractions.

Key Routes
- Kirkwall to Stromness: The main route connecting the two largest towns on the Mainland, with frequent services throughout the day.

- Kirkwall to St. Margaret's Hope: A vital route connecting Kirkwall with the ferry terminal at St. Margaret's Hope.
- Kirkwall Airport Service: A dedicated service linking Kirkwall with the airport, ensuring easy access for travelers.

Timetables and Frequency
- Regular Services: Most routes operate hourly, with more frequent services during peak times.
- Seasonal Variations: Timetables can change during the off-peak season, so it's advisable to check schedules ahead of time.

Ticketing and Passes
- Single and Return Tickets: Available for individual journeys, with prices varying based on distance.
- Day Passes: Unlimited travel on all Stagecoach buses for a fixed price, usually between £5 and £10. Ideal for exploring multiple locations in a single day.
- Weekly Passes: For extended stays, a weekly pass offers unlimited travel at a discounted rate.

Inter-Island Ferries

Orkney Ferries
- Service Provider: Orkney Ferries operates a comprehensive network of inter-island ferry

services, connecting the Mainland with the outlying islands.
- Key Routes:
  - Kirkwall to Westray and Papa Westray
  - Kirkwall to Sanday, Stronsay, and Eday
  - Houton to Lyness (Hoy) and Flotta
  - St. Margaret's Hope to South Ronaldsay

Timetables and Frequency
- Regular Services: Most islands have daily services, though frequency can vary depending on the island and time of year.
- Advance Booking: Recommended, especially during peak seasons and for vehicles.

Ticketing
- Single and Return Tickets: Prices vary based on the distance and whether you are traveling as a foot passenger or with a vehicle.
- Multi-Trip Passes: Offer savings for frequent travelers. Consider purchasing a pass if you plan to visit multiple islands.

Cycling and Walking
Bike Rentals
- Availability: Bike rentals are available in Kirkwall, Stromness, and some of the outlying islands. Rates typically range from £10 to £20 per day.

- Cycling Routes: Orkney's relatively flat terrain and scenic roads make it an ideal location for cycling. Popular routes include the Kirkwall to Stromness cycle path and island-specific trails.

Walking
- Trails and Paths: Orkney offers numerous well-marked walking trails, from coastal paths to inland routes. Walking is a great way to explore the natural beauty and historical sites.
- Guided Walks: Some local guides offer walking tours, providing insights into the history and ecology of the islands.

Taxis and Car Hire

Taxis
- Availability: Taxis are available in Kirkwall and Stromness, with services extending to other parts of the Mainland and connected islands.
- Cost: Metered fares, with additional charges for late-night or long-distance journeys. Booking in advance is recommended, especially during busy times.

Car Hire
- Rental Companies: Several car rental companies operate in Orkney, with pick-up locations at Kirkwall Airport and in town centers.

- Cost: Daily rates range from £30 to £60, depending on the vehicle type and rental duration. Book in advance to ensure availability.

Travel Tips

Plan Ahead
- Check Timetables: Schedules for buses and ferries can vary, especially during off-peak seasons. Always check current timetables before planning your journey.
- Advance Booking: For inter-island ferries and car rentals, advance booking is highly recommended, particularly in the summer months.

Use Passes
- Day and Weekly Passes: Make the most of unlimited travel passes for cost-effective and flexible travel around the islands.

Local Insights
- Ask Locals: Residents often have valuable insights into the best routes, lesser-known attractions, and travel tips.

Public transportation in Orkney is well-organized and efficient, providing a convenient way to explore the islands. Whether you're using the bus network on the Mainland, taking inter-island ferries, or enjoying the scenic routes by bike or on foot, you'll find that getting around Orkney is straightforward and enjoyable. By planning ahead and making use of available passes and services, you can navigate the islands with ease and fully experience the unique beauty and culture of Orkney.

Car Rentals And Driving Tips

Renting a car is a convenient and flexible way to explore Orkney, allowing you to visit remote sites and enjoy the stunning scenery at your own pace. Here's a comprehensive guide to car rentals and essential driving tips for visitors in Orkney.

Car Rentals in Orkney
Rental Companies
- Orkney Car Hire: A local company offering a range of vehicles from small cars to larger family vehicles.
- Avis Car Rental: Located at Kirkwall Airport, offering a variety of modern vehicles.

- Drive Orkney: Another local provider with a good selection of cars, including automatic and manual options.

Booking Tips
- Advance Booking: Reserve your vehicle well in advance, especially during peak tourist seasons, to ensure availability and secure the best rates.
- Online Reservations: Most rental companies offer online booking systems, making it easy to compare prices and choose the right vehicle for your needs.
- Airport Pickup: If you're flying into Kirkwall, consider renting a car directly from the airport for convenience.

Rental Costs
- Daily Rates: Typically range from £30 to £60 per day, depending on the vehicle type and rental duration.
- Weekly Rates: Longer rentals often come with discounted rates, so consider booking for a week if you plan an extended stay.
- Insurance: Basic insurance is usually included, but check for options to add additional coverage for peace of mind.

Requirements
- Driving License: A valid driving license from your home country is required. An International Driving

Permit (IDP) is not necessary if your license is in English.
- Age Restrictions: Most rental companies require drivers to be at least 21 years old, with a minimum of one year of driving experience. Drivers under 25 may incur a young driver surcharge.
- Credit Card: A credit card is typically required for the security deposit.

Driving Tips in Orkney

Road Conditions
- Road Types: Orkney's roads range from main highways to narrow, single-track roads with passing places. Most roads are well-maintained, but some rural routes may be less so.
- Speed Limits: The speed limit is 60 mph (97 km/h) on open roads and 30 mph (48 km/h) in towns and villages. Always adhere to posted speed limits and drive cautiously.

Navigation
- Maps and GPS: While GPS is useful, having a physical map can be handy in areas with limited signal. Orkney's road signs are generally clear and well-placed.
- Planning Routes: Plan your routes in advance, especially if you're visiting multiple islands. Check ferry schedules and book crossings ahead of time if needed.

Fuel Stations
- Availability: Fuel stations are available in Kirkwall, Stromness, and other main towns. Rural areas may have fewer stations, so fill up when you have the opportunity.
- Fuel Types: Both petrol and diesel are available. Ensure you know your vehicle's fuel type to avoid issues.

Parking
- Towns and Villages: Parking is generally free in most towns and villages, with designated car parks available. Some areas may have time restrictions, so check signs.
- Tourist Sites: Popular attractions have parking facilities, though they may fill up quickly during peak times. Arrive early to secure a spot.

Island Hopping with Your Car

Inter-Island Ferries
- Booking: Book your vehicle space on inter-island ferries well in advance, as spaces are limited. Orkney Ferries operates services to various islands.
- Ferry Costs: Costs vary based on the route and vehicle size. Multi-trip passes can offer savings if you plan to visit multiple islands.

- Boarding: Arrive early for ferry departures, as loading can take time, especially during busy periods.

Safety and Courtesy
Single-Track Roads
- Passing Places: Use designated passing places to allow oncoming traffic to pass. If a vehicle is behind you, pull over at the next passing place to let them pass.
- Sheep and Wildlife: Be aware of sheep and other wildlife on the roads, especially in rural areas. Drive slowly and be prepared to stop.

Weather Conditions
- Wind and Rain: Orkney's weather can be unpredictable. Strong winds and heavy rain can affect driving conditions, so adjust your speed and drive with caution.
- Fog and Ice: In winter, fog and icy roads can be hazardous. Ensure your vehicle is equipped for winter driving and check weather forecasts before setting out.

Local Driving Etiquette
Respect Speed Limits
- Safety First: Adhere to speed limits and drive safely, particularly in residential areas and near schools.

- Cautious Overtaking: Only overtake when it's safe to do so. Many roads are narrow, so patience is essential.

Friendly Waves
- Local Custom: It's customary to give a friendly wave to other drivers when using passing places or when they let you pass.

Renting a car in Orkney offers the freedom to explore the islands at your leisure, from historical sites and natural wonders to quaint villages and scenic coastlines. By following these tips and driving with care, you can ensure a safe and enjoyable journey throughout Orkney. Whether you're navigating the Mainland or island-hopping, a rental car provides the flexibility and convenience to make the most of your visit.

Cycling And Walking

Exploring Orkney by bike or on foot is a fantastic way to experience the islands' stunning landscapes, rich history, and vibrant wildlife up close. Whether you prefer the freedom of cycling or the pace of walking, Orkney offers numerous routes and trails suitable for all levels of fitness and interest.

Cycling in Orkney

Bike Rentals
- Availability: Bicycles can be rented from several providers in Kirkwall, Stromness, and some of the outer islands.
- Orkney Cycle Hire: Based in Stromness, offering a variety of bikes, including road bikes, hybrids, and electric bikes.
- Cycle Orkney: Located in Kirkwall, providing a range of bikes and equipment for rent.
- Pedal Power Orkney: Offering bike rentals and guided cycling tours.
- Cost: Rental rates typically range from £10 to £20 per day. Discounts are often available for longer rentals.

Popular Cycling Routes
- Kirkwall to Stromness Cycle Path: A scenic 14-mile route connecting Orkney's two largest towns. The path follows quieter roads and offers beautiful coastal views.
- West Mainland Circular Route: A 30-mile loop that takes you through picturesque villages, past historic sites like the Ring of Brodgar, and along stunning coastlines.
- East Mainland Loop: A 25-mile circuit exploring the eastern part of Mainland, including highlights like the Churchill Barriers and the Italian Chapel.

- Hoy Island: A challenging ride with rewarding views, including the dramatic cliffs and the Old Man of Hoy sea stack.

Cycling Tips
- Weather Preparedness: Orkney's weather can be unpredictable, so dress in layers and carry waterproof gear.
- Safety Gear: Always wear a helmet and use high-visibility clothing or lights, especially on rural roads.
- Road Awareness: Be mindful of single-track roads with passing places. Yield to oncoming traffic and use passing places courteously.
- Water and Snacks: Carry sufficient water and snacks, as services can be sparse in rural areas.

Walking in Orkney
Popular Walking Trails
- The St. Magnus Way: A 55-mile pilgrimage route from Egilsay to Kirkwall, inspired by the journey of Orkney's patron saint. The trail is divided into manageable sections, each offering unique landscapes and historical sites.
- West Mainland Coastal Path: A series of interconnected coastal trails offering spectacular views, wildlife watching, and visits to ancient sites like Skara Brae and the Brough of Birsay.

- Hoy's Rackwick Bay to the Old Man of Hoy: A moderately challenging 6-mile round trip with breathtaking views of the sea stack and the dramatic cliffs of Hoy.
- The Scapa Flow Trail: A gentle 7-mile walk along the coastline of Scapa Flow, with opportunities to learn about Orkney's naval history and enjoy panoramic sea views.
- Papay Peedie Sea Walk: A leisurely 4-mile loop on Papa Westray, taking in the island's rich birdlife, archaeological sites, and beautiful beaches.

Guided Walks
- Local Guides: Many local companies and guides offer walking tours, providing insights into Orkney's history, culture, and natural environment.
- Heritage Walks: Organized by the Orkney Heritage Society, these walks explore historical landmarks and offer expert commentary on Orkney's past.

Walking Tips
- Footwear: Wear sturdy, comfortable walking boots, especially for rough or uneven terrain.
- Navigation: Carry a map and compass or a GPS device. Some trails are well-marked, but others may require navigation skills.

- Weather Preparedness: Orkney's weather can change quickly. Dress in layers and bring waterproof clothing.
- Wildlife Awareness: Respect local wildlife and follow guidelines to minimize disturbance, particularly during nesting seasons.
- Safety: Inform someone of your plans before heading out, especially for longer or more remote walks. Carry a basic first aid kit and a fully charged mobile phone.

Combining Cycling and Walking
Bike-and-Hike Adventures
- Flexible Exploration: Combine cycling and walking for a versatile way to explore Orkney. Cycle to a trailhead, then hike to a scenic viewpoint or historical site.
- Island Hopping: Use inter-island ferries to transport your bike and explore multiple islands. Cycle around the islands and hike to specific attractions or viewpoints.

Tips for Combining Activities
- Lightweight Gear: Use a lightweight, portable bike lock and carry essentials in a backpack.
- Planning: Plan your routes and schedules to ensure you have enough time for both cycling and walking activities. Check ferry times in advance.

Exploring Orkney by bike or on foot offers a unique and immersive way to experience the islands' natural beauty, historical sites, and vibrant culture. With well-maintained paths, scenic routes, and ample rental options, visitors of all fitness levels can enjoy the freedom and adventure of cycling and walking in Orkney. By following the provided tips and planning your routes, you can make the most of your visit and create lasting memories of your time on these enchanting islands.

Ferry Services And Islands Hopping

Island hopping is an essential and delightful part of exploring Orkney, offering the opportunity to discover the unique character and beauty of each island. The well-organized ferry services make traveling between the islands straightforward and enjoyable. Here's a comprehensive guide to ferry services and island hopping in Orkney.

Ferry Services in Orkney
Main Operators
- Orkney Ferries: The primary ferry operator for inter-island travel within Orkney, providing reliable services to most of the inhabited islands.
- NorthLink Ferries: Operates routes between the Orkney Mainland and the Scottish mainland, as well as services to Shetland.

Key Routes
- Kirkwall to North Isles: Frequent services connecting Kirkwall with the North Isles, including Westray, Papa Westray, Sanday, Stronsay, and Eday.
- Houton to Hoy and Flotta: Regular ferries from Houton on the Orkney Mainland to Lyness on Hoy and Flotta.
- St. Margaret's Hope to South Ronaldsay: Served by Pentland Ferries, connecting the Orkney Mainland with the southern isles.
- Mainland to Rousay, Egilsay, and Wyre: Daily services from Tingwall to these nearby islands.

Booking and Schedules

Timetables
- Seasonal Variations: Ferry schedules can vary depending on the season, with more frequent services during the summer months. Always check current timetables before planning your journey.
- Online Schedules: Up-to-date timetables are available on the Orkney Ferries and NorthLink Ferries websites.

Booking Tickets
- Advance Booking: It's advisable to book ferry tickets in advance, especially during peak tourist seasons and if you're traveling with a vehicle.

- Online Booking: Most ferry operators offer online booking systems for convenience. Alternatively, tickets can be purchased at ferry terminals.

Costs and Ticket Types

Fare Structure
- Foot Passengers: Single and return fares for foot passengers are generally affordable, ranging from £5 to £15 depending on the route.
- Vehicles: Vehicle fares vary based on the size and type of vehicle, with prices typically ranging from £20 to £50 for a car. There may be additional charges for trailers or caravans.
- Multi-Trip Passes: For those planning to visit multiple islands, multi-trip passes offer cost savings and flexibility.

Onboard Facilities

Amenities
- Passenger Lounges: Comfortable seating areas with panoramic windows for enjoying the views.
- Cafes and Refreshments: Most ferries have onboard cafes offering snacks, drinks, and light meals.
- Toilets: Restroom facilities are available on all ferries.

Island Hopping Adventures

Planning Your Island Hopping

- Research Destinations: Each island has its unique attractions and character. Research in advance to decide which islands you want to visit.
- Check Ferry Times: Plan your itinerary around ferry schedules to ensure you have enough time to explore each island.
- Accommodation: If you plan to stay overnight on one of the islands, book your accommodation well in advance.

Highlights of Island Hopping in Orkney

Westray
- Attractions: Known as the "Queen of the Isles," Westray offers beautiful beaches, birdwatching opportunities, and the impressive Noltland Castle.
- Activities: Explore the Westray Heritage Centre, walk the Westside Scenic Walk, and visit the Westray Art Gallery.

Papa Westray
- Attractions: Home to the Knap of Howar, one of the oldest preserved stone houses in northern Europe.
- Activities: Enjoy birdwatching at the North Hill RSPB Reserve and explore the island's rich archaeological sites.

Hoy

- Attractions: Famous for the Old Man of Hoy sea stack and the dramatic landscape of Rackwick Bay.
- Activities: Hike to the Old Man of Hoy, visit the Scapa Flow Visitor Centre and Museum, and explore the wartime heritage of Lyness.

Sanday
- Attractions: Known for its stunning beaches, dunes, and rich wildlife.
- Activities: Visit the Sanday Heritage Centre, explore the archaeological sites, and enjoy the island's natural beauty.

Rousay
- Attractions: Often called the "Egypt of the North" due to its wealth of archaeological sites.
- Activities: Explore the Midhowe Broch, walk the Westness Heritage Walk, and visit the Trumland House Gardens.

Tips for a Smooth Island Hopping Experience
Be Prepared
- Weather: Orkney's weather can be unpredictable. Dress in layers and bring waterproof clothing.
- Essentials: Pack essentials like water, snacks, and a first aid kit, especially for longer journeys or visits to remote areas.

Respect Local Communities

- Island Etiquette: Be respectful of local communities and follow any guidelines provided by ferry operators or island authorities.
- Wildlife: Observe wildlife from a distance and follow local guidelines to minimize disturbance.

Flexibility
- Stay Flexible: Weather conditions can sometimes affect ferry schedules. Be flexible with your plans and allow extra time for travel.

Ferry services are an integral part of the Orkney experience, offering an efficient and enjoyable way to explore the archipelago's diverse islands. Whether you're visiting for the day or planning an extended island-hopping adventure, understanding the ferry system and planning your trips in advance will ensure a smooth and memorable journey. Embrace the adventure of island hopping and discover the unique charm and beauty that each island in Orkney has to offer.

Chapter 5

SLEEPING OVER

Accommodation Options

Hotels And Inns

Orkney offers a wide range of hotels and inns to suit all tastes and budgets, providing comfortable and welcoming bases from which to explore the islands. Whether you're looking for luxury, historical charm, or budget-friendly options, there's something for everyone. Here's a comprehensive guide to hotels and inns in Orkney.

Luxury and Boutique Hotels
The Kirkwall Hotel

- Location: Kirkwall
- Description: A historic hotel located in the heart of Kirkwall, overlooking the harbour. It offers elegantly decorated rooms, a fine dining restaurant, and a cozy lounge bar.
- Amenities: Free Wi-Fi, on-site restaurant, bar, room service, conference facilities.
- Nearby Attractions: St Magnus Cathedral, Orkney Museum, Highland Park Distillery.

The Lynnfield Hotel
- Location: Kirkwall
- Description: A boutique hotel set in a historic building, offering luxurious rooms and exceptional dining. Known for its warm hospitality and attention to detail.
- Amenities: Free Wi-Fi, restaurant, bar, garden, parking.
- Nearby Attractions: Scapa Flow, Orkney Museum, Italian Chapel.

The Foveran Restaurant with Rooms
- Location: St. Ola
- Description: A family-run establishment offering high-quality accommodation and award-winning cuisine. Rooms offer stunning views of Scapa Flow.
- Amenities: Free Wi-Fi, restaurant, bar, parking.
- Nearby Attractions: Scapa Beach, Orkney Brewery, Scapa Distillery.

Mid-Range Hotels

Albert Hotel
- Location: Kirkwall
- Description: A comfortable hotel in the center of Kirkwall, blending traditional charm with modern amenities. Ideal for both business and leisure travelers.
- Amenities: Free Wi-Fi, restaurant, bar, meeting rooms, parking.
- Nearby Attractions: Bishop's and Earl's Palaces, Orkney Wireless Museum, St Magnus Cathedral.

Stromness Hotel
- Location: Stromness
- Description: A historic hotel overlooking the picturesque harbor of Stromness, offering cozy rooms and a welcoming atmosphere.
- Amenities: Free Wi-Fi, restaurant, bar, meeting facilities, parking.
- Nearby Attractions: Pier Arts Centre, Ness Battery, Hoy Island.

Standing Stones Hotel
- Location: Stenness
- Description: A family-friendly hotel located near the famous Standing Stones of Stenness and the Ring of Brodgar, perfect for exploring Orkney's archaeological sites.

- Amenities: Free Wi-Fi, restaurant, bar, parking, family rooms.
- Nearby Attractions: Ring of Brodgar, Maeshowe, Skara Brae.

Budget-Friendly Hotels and Inns

Ayre Hotel and Apartments
- Location: Kirkwall
- Description: A modern and affordable hotel offering comfortable rooms and self-catering apartments, ideal for budget-conscious travelers.
- Amenities: Free Wi-Fi, restaurant, bar, parking, self-catering facilities.
- Nearby Attractions: Orkney Museum, St Magnus Cathedral, Kirkwall Marina.

Ferry Inn
- Location: Stromness
- Description: A friendly inn located in the heart of Stromness, offering affordable accommodation and a lively pub atmosphere.
- Amenities: Free Wi-Fi, restaurant, bar, parking.
- Nearby Attractions: Stromness Museum, Ness Battery, Hoy Island.

The Orcadian Hotel
- Location: Kirkwall

- Description: A budget-friendly option offering basic but comfortable accommodation with a convenient location close to Kirkwall's amenities.
- Amenities: Free Wi-Fi, bar, parking, breakfast included.
- Nearby Attractions: Highland Park Distillery, Scapa Flow, Italian Chapel.

Unique and Historic Inns

The Taversoe
- Location: Rousay
- Description: A charming inn located on the island of Rousay, known for its friendly service and stunning views over the Eynhallow Sound.
- Amenities: Free Wi-Fi, restaurant, bar, parking.
- Nearby Attractions: Midhowe Broch, Westness Heritage Walk, Trumland House Gardens.

Birsay Bay Tearoom and B&B
- Location: Birsay
- Description: A quaint establishment offering cozy rooms and a tearoom with homemade treats. Ideal for a peaceful retreat in the Orkney countryside.
- Amenities: Free Wi-Fi, tearoom, parking, breakfast included.
- Nearby Attractions: Brough of Birsay, Earl's Palace, Marwick Head.

Tips for Choosing Accommodation

Location
- Proximity to Attractions: Choose accommodation close to the sites you plan to visit to minimize travel time.
- Transport Links: Consider the availability of public transport or parking if you plan to rent a car.

Amenities
- Essential Services: Ensure the accommodation offers amenities that are important to you, such as free Wi-Fi, parking, and dining options.
- Special Requirements: Check if the hotel can accommodate any special requirements you may have, such as accessibility features or pet-friendly rooms.

Reviews and Recommendations
- Online Reviews: Read reviews on travel websites and forums to get an idea of the experiences of other travelers.
- Local Recommendations: Seek recommendations from locals or travel guides for authentic and unique accommodation options.

Orkney's hotels and inns offer a diverse range of accommodation options to suit every traveler's needs, from luxury boutique hotels to budget-friendly inns and unique historic stays. By considering your budget, preferred amenities, and desired location, you can find the perfect base for your Orkney adventure. Whether you're looking for a cozy inn with local charm or a modern hotel with all the comforts, Orkney's hospitality will ensure a memorable and enjoyable stay.

Bed And Breakfasts

Bed and breakfasts (B&Bs) offer a charming and personalized accommodation experience, often providing visitors with a warm welcome and a taste of local life. In Orkney, you'll find a wide variety of B&Bs, each with its own unique character and hospitality. Here's a comprehensive guide to some of the best bed and breakfasts for visitors in Orkney.

Why Choose a Bed and Breakfast?

- Personal Touch: B&Bs are often run by local families or individuals who offer a personal touch and insider knowledge about the area.

- Comfort and Character: Many B&Bs are set in historic buildings or picturesque locations, offering a unique and cozy atmosphere.

- Home-Cooked Breakfasts: Enjoy delicious home-cooked breakfasts featuring local produce, a great way to start your day of exploring.

Top Bed and Breakfasts in Orkney
Bellavista Guest House

- Location: Kirkwall
- Description: A well-appointed guest house with stunning views over Kirkwall Bay. It offers comfortable rooms with modern amenities and a friendly atmosphere.
- Amenities: Free Wi-Fi, en-suite bathrooms, tea/coffee making facilities, parking.
- Nearby Attractions: St Magnus Cathedral, Orkney Museum, Highland Park Distillery.
- Breakfast: Full Scottish breakfast with locally sourced ingredients.

Hammersmith Bed and Breakfast
- Location: Harray, West Mainland
- Description: Set in a traditional Orkney farmhouse, this B&B provides a peaceful retreat with beautiful countryside views. It's close to major archaeological sites.
- Amenities: Free Wi-Fi, en-suite bathrooms, garden, parking.
- Nearby Attractions: Ring of Brodgar, Skara Brae, Maeshowe.
- Breakfast: A hearty breakfast with homemade bread, local meats, and fresh eggs from their own hens.

Karrawa Guest House
- Location: Kirkwall

- Description: A family-run B&B offering warm hospitality and comfortable accommodation within walking distance of Kirkwall town center.
- Amenities: Free Wi-Fi, en-suite bathrooms, guest lounge, parking.
- Nearby Attractions: Bishop's and Earl's Palaces, Orkney Wireless Museum, Kirkwall Marina.
- Breakfast: Cooked-to-order breakfast with a variety of options, including vegetarian choices.

Westrow Lodge Bed & Breakfast
- Location: Orphir
- Description: A modern B&B with spacious rooms and stunning views of Scapa Flow. Ideal for visitors looking to explore both the Mainland and the South Isles.
- Amenities: Free Wi-Fi, en-suite bathrooms, guest lounge, parking.
- Nearby Attractions: Orphir Round Church, Scapa Flow, Italian Chapel.
- Breakfast: Full Scottish breakfast with locally sourced produce.

Avalon House
- Location: Kirkwall
- Description: A stylish and contemporary B&B offering luxurious accommodation and exceptional service. Located just a short walk from Kirkwall's main attractions.

- Amenities: Free Wi-Fi, en-suite bathrooms, guest lounge, parking.
- Nearby Attractions: St Magnus Cathedral, Orkney Museum, Highland Park Distillery.
- Breakfast: Gourmet breakfast with a selection of hot and cold options.

Unique and Quaint B&Bs

Buxa Farm Chalets and Croft House
- Location: Orphir
- Description: Located on a working farm, this B&B offers a unique rural experience with the chance to see farm animals and enjoy stunning coastal views.
- Amenities: Free Wi-Fi, en-suite bathrooms, self-catering facilities, parking.
- Nearby Attractions: Scapa Flow, Orphir Round Church, Italian Chapel.
- Breakfast: Full Scottish breakfast with fresh farm produce.

The Sands Bed and Breakfast
- Location: Burray
- Description: A beachfront B&B offering cozy accommodation with breathtaking sea views. Perfect for a tranquil getaway.
- Amenities: Free Wi-Fi, en-suite bathrooms, garden, parking.
- Nearby Attractions: Burray Fossil and Heritage Centre, Churchill Barriers, Italian Chapel.

- Breakfast: Traditional Scottish breakfast with locally sourced ingredients.

The Mill of Eyrland
- Location: Stenness
- Description: A beautifully restored former mill offering charming accommodation with original features and modern comforts.
- Amenities: Free Wi-Fi, en-suite bathrooms, guest lounge, parking.
- Nearby Attractions: Ring of Brodgar, Maeshowe, Standing Stones of Stenness.
- Breakfast: A delicious breakfast featuring homemade bread and jams, local meats, and fresh eggs.

Tips for Choosing a Bed and Breakfast
Consider Your Location
- Proximity to Attractions: Choose a B&B close to the sites you plan to visit to minimize travel time and maximize your exploration.
- Transport Links: Check the availability of public transport or parking if you plan to rent a car.

Read Reviews and Recommendations
- Online Reviews: Look for reviews on travel websites and forums to get an idea of the experiences of other guests.

- Personal Recommendations: Seek recommendations from locals or travel guides for authentic and unique accommodation options.

Check Amenities and Services
- Essential Amenities: Ensure the B&B offers amenities that are important to you, such as free Wi-Fi, en-suite bathrooms, and parking.
- Special Requirements: Confirm if the B&B can accommodate any special requirements you may have, such as dietary restrictions or accessibility needs.

Bed and breakfasts in Orkney offer a charming and personalized way to experience the islands, providing comfortable and welcoming accommodation with a local touch. Whether you're looking for a luxurious stay with gourmet breakfasts or a quaint and cozy retreat in a rural setting, there's a B&B to suit every preference and budget. By considering your location, reading reviews, and checking amenities, you can find the perfect B&B to make your visit to Orkney memorable and enjoyable. Enjoy the warm hospitality and unique character of Orkney's bed and breakfasts as you explore the beauty and history of these enchanting islands.

Hostels And Budget Stays

Orkney offers a range of affordable accommodation options, including hostels and budget stays, catering to travelers who seek comfort without breaking the bank. These options are perfect for solo adventurers, families, and groups looking to explore the islands on a budget while enjoying friendly hospitality and convenient amenities. Here's a comprehensive guide to hostels and budget stays in Orkney.

Why Choose Hostels and Budget Stays?
- Affordability: Hostels and budget stays offer cost-effective accommodation, freeing up more of your budget for exploring and activities.
- Community Atmosphere: Many hostels provide communal spaces where travelers can meet, share experiences, and even join group activities.

- Convenience: These accommodations often have central locations, making it easy to access local attractions, public transport, and amenities.

Top Hostels and Budget Stays in Orkney
Kirkwall Youth Hostel
- Location: Kirkwall
- Description: A well-equipped hostel in the heart of Kirkwall, offering a range of dormitory and private rooms. Ideal for solo travelers, families, and groups.
- Amenities: Free Wi-Fi, shared kitchen, communal lounge, laundry facilities, bike storage.
- Nearby Attractions: St Magnus Cathedral, Orkney Museum, Highland Park Distillery.
- Price Range: £20-£40 per night.

Orcades Hostel
- Location: Kirkwall
- Description: A modern and spacious hostel offering comfortable accommodation with excellent facilities. Close to Kirkwall's main attractions.
- Amenities: Free Wi-Fi, private rooms with en-suite bathrooms, communal kitchen, lounge, free parking.
- Nearby Attractions: Bishop's and Earl's Palaces, Orkney Wireless Museum, Kirkwall Marina.
- Price Range: £25-£50 per night.

Stromness Youth Hostel

- Location: Stromness
- Description: A cozy hostel located in the historic town of Stromness, providing a friendly atmosphere and easy access to local attractions.
- Amenities: Free Wi-Fi, shared kitchen, common room, laundry facilities, garden.
- Nearby Attractions: Pier Arts Centre, Ness Battery, Hoy Island.
- Price Range: £20-£40 per night.

Birsay Outdoor Centre
- Location: Birsay, West Mainland
- Description: A budget-friendly accommodation option with basic but comfortable facilities, ideal for groups and families. Located near beautiful coastal scenery and archaeological sites.
- Amenities: Shared kitchen, common room, free parking, group dormitories.
- Nearby Attractions: Brough of Birsay, Earl's Palace, Marwick Head.
- Price Range: £15-£30 per night.

Unique and Alternative Budget Stays
Orca Country Inn
- Location: St Margaret's Hope
- Description: A charming budget inn offering a range of affordable rooms and a warm, welcoming atmosphere. Great for travelers looking to explore the South Isles.

- Amenities: Free Wi-Fi, en-suite rooms, restaurant, bar, parking.
- Nearby Attractions: Churchill Barriers, Italian Chapel, Tomb of the Eagles.
- Price Range: £30-£60 per night.

Wheems Organic Farm Campsite and Bothies
- Location: South Ronaldsay
- Description: For a unique and eco-friendly stay, this organic farm offers camping facilities and cozy bothies with stunning sea views.
- Amenities: Shared kitchen, shower facilities, eco-friendly toilets, farm shop.
- Nearby Attractions: Tomb of the Eagles, Windwick Bay, St Margaret's Hope.
- Price Range: £10-£30 per night.

Aultnagar Accommodation
- Location: Kirkwall
- Description: A budget-friendly guesthouse offering comfortable rooms and a convenient location close to Kirkwall's amenities.
- Amenities: Free Wi-Fi, shared kitchen, parking, laundry facilities.
- Nearby Attractions: St Magnus Cathedral, Orkney Museum, Kirkwall Marina.
- Price Range: £25-£45 per night.

Tips for Choosing Budget Accommodation

Consider Your Needs
- Room Type: Determine whether you prefer a dormitory, private room, or a unique option like camping or a bothy.
- Facilities: Look for amenities that are important to you, such as a kitchen, laundry facilities, or bike storage.

Location
- Proximity to Attractions: Choose accommodation that is close to the sites you plan to visit to minimize travel time and costs.
- Transport Links: Consider the availability of public transport or parking if you plan to rent a car or use local buses.

Reviews and Recommendations
- Online Reviews: Check reviews on travel websites and forums to get an idea of other travelers' experiences.
- Local Advice: Seek recommendations from locals or travel guides for authentic and reliable budget stays.

Making the Most of Your Budget Stay
Utilize Communal Spaces
- Socialize: Take advantage of common areas to meet fellow travelers, share tips, and maybe even plan activities together.

- Cook Your Meals: Use the shared kitchen facilities to prepare your meals, saving money on dining out.

Explore Local Offers
- Discounts and Deals: Look out for local discounts and deals on attractions, transport, and dining that may be available to hostel guests.
- Free Activities: Engage in free or low-cost activities like hiking, beachcombing, and visiting public museums.

Hostels and budget stays in Orkney provide a cost-effective and comfortable way to explore the islands, offering a range of accommodations to suit different preferences and budgets. From centrally located youth hostels to unique farm stays, there's something for every budget-conscious traveler. By choosing the right accommodation, utilizing communal spaces, and exploring local offers, you can enjoy a memorable and affordable visit to Orkney. Embrace the friendly atmosphere and practical amenities of Orkney's budget accommodations as you discover the beauty and history of these captivating islands.

Camping And Glamping

Camping and glamping offer a unique and immersive way to experience the natural beauty of Orkney. Whether you prefer traditional camping under the stars or luxurious glamping with all the comforts of home, Orkney's landscapes provide a stunning backdrop for your outdoor adventure. Here's a comprehensive guide to camping and glamping options for visitors in Orkney.

Why Choose Camping and Glamping?
- Close to Nature: Enjoy the stunning natural scenery and wildlife of Orkney up close.
- Flexibility: Choose from a variety of locations and settings, from coastal sites to countryside retreats.
- Affordability: Camping is often a budget-friendly option, and glamping offers luxury at a fraction of the cost of a hotel.

Top Camping Sites in Orkney
Orkney Caravan Park
- Location: Kirkwall
- Description: A well-equipped campsite close to Kirkwall's amenities and attractions. Offers pitches for tents, caravans, and motorhomes.
- Amenities: Electric hook-ups, shower and toilet facilities, laundry, communal kitchen, Wi-Fi.
- Nearby Attractions: St Magnus Cathedral, Orkney Museum, Highland Park Distillery.

- Price Range: £10-£25 per night.

Wheems Organic Farm Campsite
- Location: South Ronaldsay
- Description: An eco-friendly campsite set on an organic farm, offering beautiful sea views and a peaceful atmosphere.
- Amenities: Eco-friendly toilets, hot showers, communal kitchen, farm shop, Wi-Fi.
- Nearby Attractions: Tomb of the Eagles, Windwick Bay, St Margaret's Hope.
- Price Range: £10-£20 per night.

Birsay Outdoor Centre
- Location: Birsay, West Mainland
- Description: A scenic campsite near Birsay Bay, ideal for exploring the coastal landscape and nearby archaeological sites.
- Amenities: Basic shower and toilet facilities, kitchen, communal lounge, parking.
- Nearby Attractions: Brough of Birsay, Earl's Palace, Marwick Head.
- Price Range: £10-£20 per night.

Top Glamping Sites in Orkney
The Little Bothy
- Location: Deerness

- Description: A charming glamping bothy set in a secluded rural location, offering a cozy and comfortable stay with stunning countryside views.
- Amenities: Wood-burning stove, kitchenette, en-suite bathroom, outdoor seating area, parking.
- Nearby Attractions: Mull Head Nature Reserve, Gloup, Deerness Distillery.
- Price Range: £50-£100 per night.

Orkney Staycations
- Location: St. Margaret's Hope
- Description: Luxury glamping pods equipped with modern amenities, providing a comfortable and stylish retreat.
- Amenities: En-suite bathroom, kitchenette, heating, Wi-Fi, outdoor seating area.
- Nearby Attractions: Churchill Barriers, Italian Chapel, Tomb of the Eagles.
- Price Range: £60-£120 per night.

The Peedie Lodge
- Location: Stenness
- Description: A well-appointed glamping lodge near the famous Standing Stones of Stenness, perfect for a relaxing and luxurious stay.
- Amenities: Fully equipped kitchen, en-suite bathroom, heating, Wi-Fi, private garden.
- Nearby Attractions: Ring of Brodgar, Maeshowe, Standing Stones of Stenness.

- Price Range: £70-£150 per night.

Tips for Camping and Glamping in Orkney

Be Prepared for the Weather
- Layered Clothing: Orkney's weather can be unpredictable, so pack layered clothing to stay warm and dry.
- Waterproof Gear: Bring waterproof jackets, trousers, and sturdy footwear.

Choose Your Location Wisely
- Proximity to Attractions: Select a campsite or glamping site that's close to the attractions you plan to visit.
- Facilities: Check the available facilities to ensure they meet your needs, such as shower blocks, kitchens, and Wi-Fi.

Respect the Environment
- Leave No Trace: Follow the Leave No Trace principles to minimize your impact on the environment.
- Wildlife: Observe wildlife from a distance and do not disturb their natural habitat.

Safety Tips
- Campfire Safety: If campfires are allowed, always follow safety guidelines and never leave a fire unattended.

- First Aid Kit: Carry a basic first aid kit for minor injuries and emergencies.

Making the Most of Your Camping and Glamping Experience

Engage in Outdoor Activities
- Hiking: Explore Orkney's numerous hiking trails, such as the coastal paths around Hoy or the cliffs of Yesnaby.
- Birdwatching: Bring binoculars and enjoy birdwatching at locations like the RSPB reserves on Westray and Mainland.

Enjoy the Night Sky
- Stargazing: Orkney's clear skies and low light pollution make it an excellent spot for stargazing. Bring a telescope or binoculars for a better view.

Local Produce
- Farm Shops: Purchase fresh local produce from farm shops like those at Wheems Organic Farm.
- Seafood: Try Orkney's renowned seafood, available from local markets and restaurants.

Camping and glamping in Orkney offer unique and memorable ways to experience the islands' natural beauty and charm. Whether you choose a traditional campsite or a luxurious glamping pod, you'll enjoy the stunning landscapes, rich wildlife, and serene environment that Orkney has to offer. By being prepared for the weather, respecting the environment, and making the most of outdoor activities, your camping or glamping adventure in Orkney will be an unforgettable experience. Embrace the beauty of nature and the comfort of well-equipped accommodations as you explore all that Orkney has to offer.

Best Places To Stay

Orkney offers a diverse range of accommodation options to suit every traveler's needs and preferences. From luxurious hotels to charming bed and breakfasts, cozy cottages, and budget-friendly hostels, there's something for everyone. Here's a comprehensive guide to the best places to stay in Orkney, categorized by accommodation type.

Hotels and Inns

The Kirkwall Hotel
- Location: Kirkwall
- Description: A historic hotel located on the waterfront, offering comfortable rooms and excellent service. The Kirkwall Hotel blends traditional charm with modern amenities.
- Amenities: Free Wi-Fi, en-suite bathrooms, restaurant, bar, parking.

- Nearby Attractions: St Magnus Cathedral, Orkney Museum, Highland Park Distillery.
- Price Range: £80-£150 per night.

The Orkney Hotel
- Location: Kirkwall
- Description: Situated in a 17th-century building, this hotel offers a blend of historic charm and modern comfort. It's located in the heart of Kirkwall, close to main attractions.
- Amenities: Free Wi-Fi, en-suite bathrooms, restaurant, bar, parking.
- Nearby Attractions: Bishop's and Earl's Palaces, Orkney Wireless Museum, Kirkwall Marina.
- Price Range: £90-£160 per night.

Ferry Inn
- Location: Stromness
- Description: A cozy inn located in the picturesque town of Stromness, offering comfortable accommodation and a welcoming atmosphere.
- Amenities: Free Wi-Fi, en-suite bathrooms, restaurant, bar, parking.
- Nearby Attractions: Pier Arts Centre, Ness Battery, Hoy Island.
- Price Range: £70-£130 per night.

Bed and Breakfasts

Bellavista Guest House

- Location: Kirkwall
- Description: A well-appointed guest house with stunning views over Kirkwall Bay. It offers comfortable rooms with modern amenities and a friendly atmosphere.
- Amenities: Free Wi-Fi, en-suite bathrooms, tea/coffee making facilities, parking.
- Nearby Attractions: St Magnus Cathedral, Orkney Museum, Highland Park Distillery.
- Breakfast: Full Scottish breakfast with locally sourced ingredients.
- Price Range: £60-£100 per night.

Hammersmith Bed and Breakfast
- Location: Harray, West Mainland
- Description: Set in a traditional Orkney farmhouse, this B&B provides a peaceful retreat with beautiful countryside views. It's close to major archaeological sites.
- Amenities: Free Wi-Fi, en-suite bathrooms, garden, parking.
- Nearby Attractions: Ring of Brodgar, Skara Brae, Maeshowe.
- Breakfast: A hearty breakfast with homemade bread, local meats, and fresh eggs from their own hens.
- Price Range: £50-£90 per night.

Karrawa Guest House

- Location: Kirkwall
- Description: A family-run B&B offering warm hospitality and comfortable accommodation within walking distance of Kirkwall town center.
- Amenities: Free Wi-Fi, en-suite bathrooms, guest lounge, parking.
- Nearby Attractions: Bishop's and Earl's Palaces, Orkney Wireless Museum, Kirkwall Marina.
- Breakfast: Cooked-to-order breakfast with a variety of options, including vegetarian choices.
- Price Range: £55-£95 per night.

Cottages and Self-Catering
Orkney Cottages
- Location: Various locations across Orkney
- Description: Offering a range of self-catering cottages, from traditional stone cottages to modern holiday homes, these accommodations provide flexibility and comfort.
- Amenities: Fully equipped kitchens, living areas, bathrooms, parking, Wi-Fi.
- Nearby Attractions: Depending on location, close to major sites like Skara Brae, Ring of Brodgar, and Italian Chapel.
- Price Range: £300-£700 per week.

Foinhaven Bed and Breakfast & Self-Catering
- Location: Stromness

- Description: Offers both B&B rooms and a self-catering apartment. Located in Stromness, providing easy access to local attractions.
- Amenities: Free Wi-Fi, en-suite bathrooms, kitchen facilities, parking.
- Nearby Attractions: Pier Arts Centre, Ness Battery, Hoy Island.
- Breakfast: Available for B&B guests, featuring local produce.
- Price Range: £50-£90 per night (B&B), £400-£600 per week (self-catering).

Hostels and Budget Stays

Kirkwall Youth Hostel
- Location: Kirkwall
- Description: A well-equipped hostel in the heart of Kirkwall, offering a range of dormitory and private rooms. Ideal for solo travelers, families, and groups.
- Amenities: Free Wi-Fi, shared kitchen, communal lounge, laundry facilities, bike storage.
- Nearby Attractions: St Magnus Cathedral, Orkney Museum, Highland Park Distillery.
- Price Range: £20-£40 per night.

Orcades Hostel
- Location: Kirkwall
- Description: A modern and spacious hostel offering comfortable accommodation with excellent facilities. Close to Kirkwall's main attractions.

- Amenities: Free Wi-Fi, private rooms with en-suite bathrooms, communal kitchen, lounge, free parking.
- Nearby Attractions: Bishop's and Earl's Palaces, Orkney Wireless Museum, Kirkwall Marina.
- Price Range: £25-£50 per night.

Stromness Youth Hostel
- Location: Stromness
- Description: A cozy hostel located in the historic town of Stromness, providing a friendly atmosphere and easy access to local attractions.
- Amenities: Free Wi-Fi, shared kitchen, common room, laundry facilities, garden.
- Nearby Attractions: Pier Arts Centre, Ness Battery, Hoy Island.
- Price Range: £20-£40 per night.

Camping and Glamping

Orkney Caravan Park
- Location: Kirkwall
- Description: A well-equipped campsite close to Kirkwall's amenities and attractions. Offers pitches for tents, caravans, and motorhomes.
- Amenities: Electric hook-ups, shower and toilet facilities, laundry, communal kitchen, Wi-Fi.
- Nearby Attractions: St Magnus Cathedral, Orkney Museum, Highland Park Distillery.
- Price Range: £10-£25 per night.

Wheems Organic Farm Campsite
- Location: South Ronaldsay
- Description: An eco-friendly campsite set on an organic farm, offering beautiful sea views and a peaceful atmosphere.
- Amenities: Eco-friendly toilets, hot showers, communal kitchen, farm shop, Wi-Fi.
- Nearby Attractions: Tomb of the Eagles, Windwick Bay, St Margaret's Hope.
- Price Range: £10-£20 per night.

The Little Bothy
- Location: Deerness
- Description: A charming glamping bothy set in a secluded rural location, offering a cozy and comfortable stay with stunning countryside views.
- Amenities: Wood-burning stove, kitchenette, en-suite bathroom, outdoor seating area, parking.
- Nearby Attractions: Mull Head Nature Reserve, Gloup, Deerness Distillery.
- Price Range: £50-£100 per night.

Orkney offers a wide range of accommodation options to suit every traveler's needs and budget. Whether you're looking for luxurious hotels, charming bed and breakfasts, cozy cottages, budget-friendly hostels, or outdoor adventures with camping and glamping, you'll find the perfect place to stay. Each accommodation type offers unique experiences and amenities, ensuring a comfortable and enjoyable visit to the beautiful Orkney Islands. Explore the rich history, stunning landscapes, and vibrant culture of Orkney while staying in accommodations that best suit your preferences and budget.

Booking Tips And Advice

Booking accommodation in Orkney can be a seamless experience if you plan ahead and consider a few key factors. Whether you're seeking luxury, charm, budget-friendly options, or unique stays like camping and glamping, these tips will help ensure you secure the best places to stay for your visit to the Orkney Islands.

1. Plan Ahead and Book Early

Peak Season Considerations

- Summer Months: Orkney's peak tourist season is from May to September. Accommodations can fill up quickly, so it's advisable to book several months in advance.
- Festivals and Events: During popular events such as the Orkney Folk Festival and the St. Magnus Festival, accommodations can be in high demand.

Off-Peak Season

- Winter Visits: Visiting during the off-peak season can offer more availability and potentially lower prices. However, some accommodations may be closed during winter months.

2. Choose the Right Location
Proximity to Attractions
- Kirkwall and Stromness: These towns are central hubs with many attractions, dining options, and transport links. Ideal for first-time visitors.
- Remote Areas: For a more secluded experience, consider staying in smaller villages or on the outer islands, keeping in mind transportation logistics.

3. Set Your Budget and Preferences
Accommodation Types
- Luxury vs. Budget: Determine your budget and decide if you prefer luxury hotels, mid-range B&Bs, budget hostels, or camping.
- Special Requirements: Consider any special requirements such as pet-friendly accommodations, family rooms, or accessibility needs.

4. Utilize Online Booking Platforms
Reliable Websites
- Booking.com and Airbnb: These platforms offer a wide range of accommodation options with user reviews and secure booking processes.

- VisitScotland: The official tourism website provides listings of accredited accommodations in Orkney.

Reviews and Ratings
- Read Reviews: Check multiple reviews to get an accurate picture of the accommodation's quality and service.
- Star Ratings: Pay attention to star ratings and awards that indicate high standards.

5. Check for Special Offers and Deals
Seasonal Discounts
- Off-Peak Discounts: Look for discounts and special offers during the off-peak season.
- Extended Stay Offers: Some accommodations offer discounts for longer stays, typically a week or more.

Package Deals
- Accommodation and Tours: Some hotels and B&Bs offer packages that include tours or activities, providing good value for money.

6. Communicate Directly with Accommodation Providers
Confirm Details

- Special Requests: Contact the accommodation directly to confirm availability of specific amenities or to make special requests.
- Check Policies: Verify cancellation policies, check-in and check-out times, and any additional fees.

Personalized Service
- Local Recommendations: Providers can offer valuable local insights and recommendations for your stay.

7. Be Aware of Local Events and Availability

Major Events
- Festivals: Book well in advance if your visit coincides with major festivals to avoid disappointment.
- Local Celebrations: Check for local events that might impact availability or enhance your visit.

8. Consider Alternative Accommodation Options

Farm Stays and Bothies
- Unique Experiences: Explore options like farm stays, bothies, or eco-friendly lodges for a unique experience.
- Availability: These options can be popular and might require earlier booking.

9. Use Loyalty Programs and Membership Discounts

Hotel Chains

- Loyalty Programs: If you frequently use a particular hotel chain, check for loyalty programs that offer discounts or benefits.

Membership Discounts
- AAA, AARP, and Others: Utilize membership discounts if you are part of organizations that offer travel benefits.

10. Prepare for Your Stay

Arrival Time
- Late Check-In: If you're arriving late, inform the accommodation provider in advance to ensure smooth check-in.
- Early Check-Out: If you need to leave early, clarify the procedure for check-out to avoid any last-minute issues.

Packing Essentials
- Local Climate: Pack appropriately for Orkney's climate, which can be unpredictable. Layers and waterproof clothing are advisable.

Booking accommodation in Orkney requires some planning, especially during peak tourist seasons and major events. By setting your budget, choosing the right location, utilizing reliable booking platforms, and communicating directly with accommodation providers, you can secure the best options for your stay. Consider alternative and unique accommodations for a memorable experience, and take advantage of special offers and membership discounts. With these tips and advice, you'll be well-prepared to enjoy your visit to the beautiful Orkney Islands, ensuring a comfortable and enjoyable stay.

Chapter 6

EATING AND ADVENTURES

Local Cuisine And Must-try Dishes

Orkney's rich culinary heritage is deeply rooted in its natural environment, with the surrounding seas and fertile lands providing an abundance of fresh, high-quality ingredients. From succulent seafood to locally reared meat and traditional baked goods, the islands offer a gastronomic experience that reflects their unique culture and history. Here's a comprehensive guide to Orkney's local cuisine and must-try dishes for visitors.

1. Seafood Delicacies

Orkney Scallops
- Description: Orkney is renowned for its scallops, which are harvested from the clear, cold waters

around the islands. These tender and flavorful shellfish are often served pan-seared or in a delicate sauce.
- Where to Try: Many local restaurants, such as The Foveran and Helgi's, feature Orkney scallops on their menus.

Orkney Crab
- Description: The local crab is known for its sweet and succulent meat. It's typically served in salads, sandwiches, or simply enjoyed on its own with a touch of lemon.
- Where to Try: The Creel in St. Margaret's Hope and The Ferry Inn in Stromness are excellent places to enjoy Orkney crab.

Smoked Salmon
- Description: Orkney smoked salmon is famed for its rich flavor and silky texture. The fish is traditionally smoked using local hardwoods, giving it a distinctive taste.
- Where to Try: Pick up some Orkney smoked salmon from Jolly's of Orkney or visit Judith Glue Real Food Café in Kirkwall for a taste.

2. Meat and Game
Orkney Beef
- Description: Orkney beef is raised on the lush pastures of the islands and is prized for its quality

and flavor. It's often featured in hearty dishes such as roasts and steaks.

- Where to Try: Many local eateries, including The Lynnfield Hotel in Kirkwall, serve Orkney beef dishes.

Orkney Lamb

- Description: The islands' lamb is known for its tender and flavorful meat, thanks to the sheep's diet of wild herbs and grasses. It's commonly served roasted or in stews.
- Where to Try: The Foveran Restaurant offers a superb lamb dish that showcases the best of Orkney produce.

3. Dairy Products

Orkney Cheese

- Description: Orkney is home to several award-winning cheeses, including the rich and creamy Orkney Cheddar. Another popular variety is the tangy and crumbly Orkney Blue.
- Where to Try: Visit The Orkney Cheese Company for a tour and tasting, or sample local cheeses at Kirkwall's The Brig Larder.

Orkney Ice Cream

- Description: Made with fresh local milk and cream, Orkney ice cream is a treat not to be missed.

It comes in a variety of flavors, from traditional vanilla to more adventurous options.
- Where to Try: Head to Crantit Dairy in Kirkwall for some delicious Orkney ice cream.

4. Baked Goods
Beremeal Bannocks
- Description: Beremeal is a traditional Orkney flour made from an ancient variety of barley. Bannocks are a type of flatbread made from this flour, often enjoyed with butter or cheese.
- Where to Try: Try bannocks at local bakeries such as Argo's Bakery in Stromness.

Orkney Fudge
- Description: Orkney fudge is a rich and creamy confection, made using traditional recipes. It's available in a variety of flavors, including vanilla, chocolate, and whisky.
- Where to Try: Orkney Fudge Company in Stromness offers a wide selection of this delectable treat.

5. Beverages
Highland Park Whisky
- Description: Highland Park is one of the world's oldest distilleries, producing a range of single malt whiskies known for their balanced and smoky flavors.

- Where to Try: Take a distillery tour at Highland Park in Kirkwall to sample their whiskies.

Orkney Brewery Ales
- Description: The Orkney Brewery produces a range of craft beers, including the popular Dark Island and Red MacGregor ales.
- Where to Try: Visit the brewery in Quoyloo or enjoy a pint at local pubs like The Shore in Kirkwall.

Orkney Gin
- Description: Local gin distilleries, such as Orkney Distilling, create unique gins infused with local botanicals, offering a taste of the islands in every sip.
- Where to Try: Visit Orkney Distilling in Kirkwall for a tour and tasting session.

6. Traditional Dishes

Clapshot
- Description: Clapshot is a traditional Orkney dish made from mashed potatoes and neeps (swede), often served as a side dish with haggis or meat.
- Where to Try: Many local restaurants and pubs serve clapshot as part of their traditional fare.

Skirlie

- Description: Skirlie is a savory dish made from oatmeal, onions, and beef dripping. It's typically used as a stuffing for poultry or served as a side dish.
- Where to Try: Enjoy skirlie at traditional dining spots such as The Lynnfield Hotel.

Cullen Skink
- Description: A hearty Scottish soup made with smoked haddock, potatoes, and onions. It's a warming and satisfying dish perfect for chilly Orkney days.
- Where to Try: The Foveran Restaurant and Helgi's in Kirkwall both offer excellent versions of Cullen Skink.

Orkney's local cuisine is a delightful blend of fresh, high-quality ingredients and traditional recipes that reflect the islands' rich cultural heritage. From the succulent seafood and premium meats to the delicious dairy products and traditional baked goods, there's something to satisfy every palate. Be sure to explore the culinary offerings of Orkney and enjoy the unique flavors that make dining here an unforgettable experience. Whether you're dining in a fine restaurant, enjoying a casual meal at a local café, or sampling treats from a farmers' market, Orkney's food scene promises to be a highlight of your visit.

Top Restaurants And Cafes

Orkney boasts a vibrant culinary scene with a variety of restaurants and cafés that highlight the islands' fresh, local ingredients and unique flavors. Whether you're seeking traditional Orkney cuisine, seafood delicacies, or international dishes, these top dining establishments offer exceptional food and welcoming atmospheres for visitors to enjoy.

1. Restaurants
The Foveran Restaurant
- Location: Kirkwall
- Description: Known for its commitment to using local, seasonal ingredients, The Foveran offers a fine dining experience with a focus on Orkney produce. The menu changes regularly to showcase the best of the islands' bounty.

- Specialties: Orkney beef and lamb dishes, seafood platters, and creative desserts.
- Reservations: Recommended, especially during peak tourist seasons.
- Website: [The Foveran Restaurant](https://www.thefoveran.com/)

Helgi's
- Location: Kirkwall
- Description: A popular dining spot housed in a historic building with a cozy atmosphere. Helgi's offers a diverse menu featuring both traditional Orkney dishes and international cuisine.
- Specialties: Orkney seafood, steaks, vegetarian options, and homemade desserts.
- Reservations: Advisable, especially for dinner.
- Website: [Helgi's](https://www.helgis.co.uk/)

The Creel Restaurant
- Location: St. Margaret's Hope
- Description: Situated in a picturesque coastal village, The Creel specializes in seafood dishes crafted from locally sourced ingredients. It offers stunning views of the harbor.
- Specialties: Orkney crab, scallops, fish chowder, and seasonal seafood platters.
- Reservations: Recommended, particularly for waterfront seating.

- Website: [The Creel Restaurant](https://www.thecreel.co.uk/)

The Storehouse
- Location: Stromness
- Description: Located in a historic building overlooking Stromness Harbor, The Storehouse serves a menu inspired by Orkney's land and sea. It features a relaxed atmosphere with indoor and outdoor dining options.
- Specialties: Orkney beef burgers, fresh fish dishes, salads, and homemade cakes.
- Reservations: Walk-ins welcome, but reservations recommended for peak times.
- Website: [The Storehouse](https://www.thestorehousestomness.com/)

The Sands Hotel Restaurant
- Location: Burray
- Description: Offering panoramic views over Scapa Flow, The Sands Hotel Restaurant combines elegant dining with a focus on local ingredients. It's a perfect spot for both lunch and dinner.
- Specialties: Orkney lamb, seafood platters, vegetarian options, and decadent desserts.
- Reservations: Recommended, especially for dinner to enjoy sunset views.

- Website: [The Sands Hotel](https://www.thesandshotel.co.uk/)

2. Cafés and Casual Dining

Judith Glue Real Food Café
- Location: Kirkwall
- Description: A popular café and gift shop specializing in locally sourced food and crafts. Judith Glue's café offers a cozy setting to enjoy homemade soups, sandwiches, and baked goods.
- Specialties: Orkney cheese platters, smoked salmon sandwiches, Orkney fudge, and artisanal coffee.
- Seating: Walk-ins welcome, but can get busy during peak hours.
- Website: [Judith Glue Real Food Café](https://www.judithglue.com/)

The Peedie Kirk Café
- Location: St. Margaret's Hope
- Description: Located in a converted church, The Peedie Kirk Café offers a unique setting with a warm ambiance. It's known for its delicious homemade cakes, light lunches, and friendly service.
- Specialties: Orkney crab sandwiches, soup of the day, scones with Orkney butter and jam.
- Seating: Limited indoor seating with additional outdoor seating available in good weather.

- Facebook Page: [The Peedie Kirk Café](https://www.facebook.com/peediekirkcafe/)

The Reel
- Location: Kirkwall
- Description: A café and bar located near the harbor, The Reel is a popular spot for both locals and visitors. It offers a relaxed atmosphere with a menu that includes hearty meals and lighter fare.
- Specialties: Fish and chips, burgers, homemade pies, and a selection of local beers and ales.
- Seating: Walk-ins welcome, with indoor and outdoor seating options available.
- Facebook Page: [The Reel](https://www.facebook.com/thereelkirkwall/)

3. Pubs and Traditional Dining

The Stromness Hotel Restaurant
- Location: Stromness
- Description: Situated in the heart of Stromness, The Stromness Hotel Restaurant offers traditional pub dining with a focus on local ingredients. It's a cozy spot to enjoy hearty meals and friendly hospitality.
- Specialties: Orkney beef stew, haggis neeps and tatties, fresh seafood dishes, and sticky toffee pudding.
- Reservations: Recommended, especially during peak times.

- Website: [The Stromness Hotel](https://www.stromnesshotel.com/)

The Ferry Inn
- Location: Stromness
- Description: Overlooking the harbor, The Ferry Inn combines a pub atmosphere with a restaurant setting. It's known for its seafood dishes and welcoming environment.
- Specialties: Orkney crab, fisherman's pie, steaks, and homemade desserts.
- Seating: Walk-ins welcome, with indoor and outdoor seating available.
- Website: [The Ferry Inn](https://www.theferryinnstromness.co.uk/)

Orkney offers an array of dining options to suit every taste and preference, from fine dining restaurants showcasing local produce to cozy cafés serving homemade treats. Whether you're exploring Kirkwall, Stromness, or the smaller villages, you'll find delicious meals crafted from Orkney's finest ingredients. Enjoy the warm hospitality and culinary delights that make dining out in Orkney a memorable part of your visit to the islands.

Farmers Markets And Food Festivals

Orkney's vibrant food scene extends beyond restaurants and cafes to include farmers' markets and food festivals, offering visitors a chance to experience local produce and culinary delights. Here's a guide to farmers' markets and food festivals that visitors can explore in Orkney:

Farmers' Markets

Orkney Farmers' Market

- Location: Kirkwall (typically held at the Old Auction Mart)
- Description: The Orkney Farmers' Market showcases a variety of locally produced goods, including fresh vegetables, meats, seafood, cheeses, baked goods, and crafts. It's an excellent place to meet local producers and artisans.
- Opening Hours: Usually held on select Saturdays from morning to early afternoon.
- Additional Information: Check local listings or tourism websites for current schedules and vendor details.

Stromness Farmers' Market
- Location: Stromness (various locations, often in the town center)
- Description: Similar to the Kirkwall market, the Stromness Farmers' Market offers a range of locally

grown and crafted products, emphasizing fresh foods and unique Orkney specialties.
- Opening Hours: Occurs on selected dates, usually on weekends.
- Additional Information: Dates and times may vary, so it's advisable to check ahead of your visit.

Food Festivals
Orkney Food and Drink Festival
- Location: Various locations across Orkney (including Kirkwall and Stromness)
- Description: Held annually, the Orkney Food and Drink Festival celebrates the islands' culinary heritage with a series of events, tastings, demonstrations, and workshops. Visitors can sample local dishes, attend cooking classes, and enjoy live entertainment.
- Dates: Typically held in September.
- Highlights: Meet local chefs and producers, participate in food-themed tours, and discover new flavors unique to Orkney.
- Website: Check the official Orkney Food and Drink Festival website for current event details and schedules.

St. Magnus Festival Market
- Location: Kirkwall (various locations around the town)

- Description: As part of the annual St. Magnus Festival, a market often accompanies the cultural festivities. It features local food stalls, arts, crafts, and performances, providing a vibrant atmosphere for locals and visitors alike.
- Dates: Occurs during the St. Magnus Festival, typically held in June.
- Highlights: Enjoy a blend of cultural experiences with food offerings, live music, and traditional Orcadian arts.
- Website: Visit the St. Magnus Festival website for up-to-date information on the market and festival events.

Tips for Visitors
- Plan Ahead: Check local event calendars and tourism websites to confirm dates and locations of farmers' markets and food festivals during your visit.
- Sampling Local Flavors: Farmers' markets are ideal for tasting fresh, seasonal produce and artisanal products unique to Orkney.
- Cultural Experience: Food festivals offer insight into Orkney's culinary traditions, providing opportunities to engage with local chefs, producers, and artists.
- Support Local: Purchasing from farmers' markets supports local growers and artisans, ensuring sustainable practices and quality products.

Exploring farmers' markets and food festivals in Orkney is a delightful way for visitors to immerse themselves in the islands' food culture. Whether you're browsing stalls of fresh produce, sampling local delicacies, or enjoying festivities with live music and entertainment, these events offer memorable experiences that showcase the best of Orkney's culinary scene. Plan your visit to coincide with these events to savor the flavors and hospitality that make Orkney a unique destination for food enthusiasts.

Outdoor Adventures

Hiking Trails

Orkney offers a wealth of hiking opportunities, with trails that traverse its rugged coastline, rolling hills, and ancient sites. Hiking in Orkney allows visitors to experience the islands' natural beauty, rich history, and diverse wildlife up close. Here's a guide to some of the best hiking trails in Orkney for outdoor enthusiasts.

1. The Old Man of Hoy Walk
Overview
- Location: Hoy Island
- Distance: Approximately 6 miles (9.7 km) round trip
- Difficulty: Moderate to challenging
- Highlights: The iconic sea stack, dramatic coastal cliffs, and panoramic views.

Trail Description
Starting from the village of Rackwick, this trail leads hikers through the stunning landscape of Hoy, the second largest of the Orkney Islands. The path winds through heather moorland and along the rugged coastline, culminating in a spectacular view of the Old Man of Hoy, a 449-foot (137-meter) sea stack. The hike provides opportunities to spot seabirds and other wildlife, and the breathtaking scenery makes it a must-do for adventurous visitors.

2. The Gloup and Mull Head Walk
Overview
- Location: Deerness, Mainland Orkney

- Distance: Approximately 5 miles (8 km) round trip
- Difficulty: Moderate
- Highlights: The Gloup sea cave, Mull Head Nature Reserve, and coastal views.

Trail Description
This trail begins at the Mull Head car park and takes hikers through the Mull Head Nature Reserve, known for its dramatic cliffs and diverse birdlife. The walk includes a visit to the Gloup, a collapsed sea cave that offers stunning geological features. The route continues along the coast, providing expansive views of the North Sea and opportunities to see puffins, seals, and other wildlife. Interpretive signs along the way offer insights into the area's natural history.

3. The Brough of Birsay Walk
Overview
- Location: Birsay, Mainland Orkney
- Distance: Approximately 2 miles (3.2 km) round trip
- Difficulty: Easy to moderate
- Highlights: Tidal island, Pictish and Norse ruins, and seabird colonies.

Trail Description
Accessible only at low tide via a causeway, the Brough of Birsay is a small tidal island rich in

history. The walk takes visitors across the causeway to explore the remains of a Pictish and Norse settlement, including a church and various ruins. The island is also a prime spot for birdwatching, with puffins, guillemots, and fulmars nesting on the cliffs. The surrounding views of the coastline and the Atlantic Ocean are spectacular, making this an enjoyable and educational hike.

4. The Yesnaby Coastal Walk
Overview
- Location: West Mainland Orkney
- Distance: Approximately 4 miles (6.4 km) round trip
- Difficulty: Moderate
- Highlights: Dramatic cliffs, sea stacks, and rare wildflowers.

Trail Description
Starting from the Yesnaby car park, this trail follows the rugged coastline along some of Orkney's most striking cliffs. The path passes by the Yesnaby Castle sea stack and offers stunning views of the Atlantic Ocean. This area is also home to rare wildflowers, including the Scottish Primrose, which can be seen in the summer months. The walk is relatively easy but does involve some uneven terrain, so sturdy footwear is recommended.

5. The St. Magnus Way

Overview
- Location: Mainland Orkney, starting at Evie and ending at Kirkwall
- Distance: Approximately 55 miles (88 km) in total
- Difficulty: Moderate to challenging
- Highlights: Historical sites, varied landscapes, and cultural heritage.

Trail Description
The St. Magnus Way is a pilgrimage route that commemorates St. Magnus, Orkney's patron saint. The trail is divided into sections, allowing hikers to complete the walk in stages or as a multi-day trek. The route passes through diverse landscapes, including moorland, farmland, and coastal areas, and visits several historical sites such as the Broch of Gurness and St. Magnus Cathedral. Interpretive panels along the way provide information about the history and significance of each location.

Tips for Hikers
Prepare for the Weather
- Layers: Orkney's weather can be unpredictable, so dress in layers to stay comfortable.
- Waterproofs: Bring waterproof clothing and sturdy hiking boots, as the trails can be wet and muddy.

Respect the Environment

- Leave No Trace: Follow the Leave No Trace principles to protect the natural beauty of Orkney.
- Wildlife: Keep a respectful distance from wildlife, and avoid disturbing nesting birds.

Navigation and Safety
- Maps and Guides: Carry a map and guidebook, and consider using a GPS device or smartphone app for navigation.
- Safety: Let someone know your hiking plans, especially if you're heading to remote areas.

Hiking in Orkney offers an unparalleled opportunity to explore the islands' stunning landscapes, rich history, and diverse wildlife. From the dramatic sea cliffs of Hoy to the serene tidal island of Birsay, each trail provides a unique adventure. Whether you're a seasoned hiker or a casual walker, Orkney's trails promise memorable experiences and breathtaking views. Equip yourself with the right gear, respect the natural environment, and enjoy the outdoor wonders that make Orkney a hiker's paradise.

Wildlife Watching

Orkney is a haven for wildlife enthusiasts, offering unparalleled opportunities to observe a diverse array of species in their natural habitats. The islands' unique geography, rich ecosystems, and coastal landscapes provide ideal conditions for birdwatching, marine life spotting, and discovering native mammals. Here's a comprehensive guide to wildlife watching in Orkney for visitors.

1. Birdwatching in Orkney
Key Bird Species
- Puffins: These charismatic seabirds can be seen nesting on cliffs and rocky outcrops, particularly on the islands of Westray and Hoy.
- Hen Harriers: Look out for these birds of prey soaring over the moorlands, especially in the RSPB reserves.
- Red-throated Divers: Often seen on inland lochs and coastal waters, these striking birds are a highlight for birdwatchers.
- Gannets: The cliffs of Noup Head on Westray host large colonies of gannets, providing spectacular viewing opportunities.

Top Birdwatching Locations
- Marwick Head RSPB Reserve: Located on Mainland, this reserve offers dramatic cliffs teeming with seabirds, including guillemots, razorbills, and puffins.
- Broch of Birsay: A tidal island with excellent birdwatching, including puffins and skuas, accessible at low tide.

- Eynhallow Sound: A prime location for spotting migratory birds and seabirds, with boat tours available for closer views.

2. Marine Life Spotting
Key Marine Species
- Orcas (Killer Whales): These majestic creatures are often sighted around the Orkney coast, especially in the summer months.
- Seals: Both common and grey seals can be seen basking on beaches and rocks, with large colonies around the islands.
- Porpoises and Dolphins: These playful marine mammals are frequently spotted from shore and during boat trips.
- Basking Sharks: These gentle giants, the second-largest fish in the world, can occasionally be seen in Orkney's waters.

Top Marine Life Locations
- Brough of Birsay: At low tide, the waters around the island offer excellent opportunities to spot seals and seabirds.
- Scapa Flow: A renowned spot for marine life, including seals, orcas, and various seabirds. Boat tours provide the best vantage points.
- Hoxa Head: Located on South Ronaldsay, this area is known for orca sightings and offers dramatic coastal views.

3. Native Mammals

Key Mammal Species

- Otters: These elusive creatures can be found along the coastline and in freshwater habitats, particularly around the sheltered bays and lochs.
- Mountain Hares: Found on the hills of Hoy, these hares turn white in winter, blending with the snowy landscape.
- Orkney Vole: A unique subspecies of vole found only in Orkney, best spotted in the grasslands and wetlands of the islands.

Top Mammal Watching Locations
- Hoy: The rugged terrain and moorlands of Hoy are prime habitats for mountain hares and otters.
- Rousay: Known as the "Egypt of the North" for its archaeological sites, Rousay also offers good chances to see otters and voles.

Wildlife Watching Tips

Best Times to Visit
- Spring and Summer: These seasons offer the best wildlife viewing opportunities, with many bird species nesting and marine life more active.
- Early Morning and Late Evening: Wildlife is often more active during these times, making it ideal for spotting mammals and birds.

Equipment to Bring
- Binoculars: Essential for birdwatching and spotting distant marine life.
- Camera: A good quality camera with a zoom lens will help capture the stunning wildlife and landscapes.
- Field Guides: Bring a field guide to Orkney's wildlife to help identify species and learn more about their habitats.

Responsible Wildlife Watching
- Respect Wildlife: Keep a safe distance to avoid disturbing animals, especially during breeding and nesting seasons.
- Follow Guidelines: Stick to designated paths and viewing areas, and follow any guidelines provided by local wildlife organizations.
- Leave No Trace: Take all litter with you and avoid damaging natural habitats.

Wildlife Tours and Guides
Guided Tours
- Wild Orkney: Offers guided wildlife tours, including birdwatching walks and marine life boat trips. Local experts provide insights into the islands' ecosystems and species.
- Orkney Nature Tours: Specializes in customized wildlife tours, tailored to visitors' interests and

schedules. Includes opportunities for photography and detailed wildlife observation.

Self-Guided Tours
- Nature Reserves: Visit Orkney's numerous nature reserves, such as the RSPB reserves at Marwick Head and Mull Head, for self-guided wildlife watching.
- Walking Trails: Explore the islands' coastal paths and inland trails, many of which offer excellent opportunities to see a variety of wildlife.

Orkney's rich biodiversity and stunning landscapes make it a prime destination for wildlife enthusiasts. From the cliffs teeming with seabirds to the waters frequented by orcas and seals, the islands offer diverse habitats and abundant species. Whether you're an avid birdwatcher, a marine life enthusiast, or simply enjoy exploring nature, Orkney's wildlife watching opportunities promise unforgettable encounters. Equip yourself with the right gear, respect the natural environment, and immerse yourself in the wild beauty of Orkney.

Water Sports

Orkney's unique coastal environment and clear waters make it an ideal destination for water sports enthusiasts. From kayaking through sheltered bays to diving among historical shipwrecks, Orkney offers a variety of aquatic adventures for visitors of all skill levels. Here's a comprehensive guide to the best water sports activities in Orkney.

1. Kayaking and Canoeing

Overview

Kayaking and canoeing in Orkney provide a unique perspective on the islands' stunning coastline, sea caves, and marine life. Whether you prefer calm, sheltered waters or the thrill of open sea paddling, Orkney has something to offer.

Top Spots for Kayaking and Canoeing

- Scapa Flow: Known for its historical significance and tranquil waters, Scapa Flow is ideal for paddlers of all levels. Explore WWII wrecks and spot wildlife such as seals and seabirds.
- Stromness to Yesnaby: For more experienced kayakers, this route offers dramatic cliffs, sea stacks, and potential sightings of marine wildlife.
- Kirkwall Bay: A great spot for beginners, Kirkwall Bay's calm waters provide a safe environment to learn and practice paddling skills.

Guided Tours and Rentals
- Orkney Sea Kayaking: Offers guided tours and rentals, catering to all skill levels. Experienced guides provide safety instructions and insight into local history and wildlife.
- Orkney Kayak Club: Provides equipment rentals and organizes group paddles and training sessions for both locals and visitors.

2. Diving
Overview
Orkney is renowned for its world-class diving sites, particularly around Scapa Flow, one of the top wreck diving locations globally. Divers can explore sunken warships from the German High Seas Fleet, which were scuttled here in 1919, as well as other fascinating underwater sites.

Top Diving Sites
- Scapa Flow: Home to several notable wrecks, including the battleships SMS Markgraf and SMS Kronprinz Wilhelm. Suitable for advanced divers, these wrecks offer a glimpse into maritime history.
- Churchill Barriers: These causeways, built during WWII, provide exciting dive sites with smaller wrecks and abundant marine life.
- The Churchill Wrecks: For less experienced divers, these shallower wrecks offer accessible and interesting dives with varied marine life.

Dive Centers and Services
- Scapa Scuba: Offers guided dives, equipment rental, and dive training courses. Their experienced instructors provide safe and informative diving experiences.
- Radiant Queen Charters: Specializes in diving charters to the wrecks of Scapa Flow, catering to both recreational and technical divers.

3. Sailing
Overview
Sailing in Orkney allows visitors to experience the islands' scenic beauty and rich maritime heritage from the water. Whether you prefer leisurely cruises or competitive racing, Orkney's waters offer diverse sailing opportunities.

Top Sailing Areas
- Kirkwall Bay: Ideal for beginners and leisure sailors, the calm waters of Kirkwall Bay provide a scenic and relaxing sailing experience.
- Scapa Flow: Suitable for more experienced sailors, this historic natural harbor offers challenging conditions and stunning views.
- Stromness Harbour: A bustling harbor with facilities for visiting yachts and a gateway to exploring the west coast of Orkney.

Sailing Clubs and Charters
- Orkney Sailing Club: Based in Kirkwall, the club offers sailing courses, organizes races, and provides mooring facilities for visiting yachts.
- Orkney Marinas: Provides mooring facilities and services for visiting sailors in Kirkwall, Stromness, and Westray. Information on local sailing conditions and charter options is available.

4. Surfing and Windsurfing
Overview
Orkney's rugged coastline and powerful Atlantic swells make it a prime location for surfing and windsurfing. While the conditions can be challenging, they offer thrilling experiences for adventurous water sports enthusiasts.

Top Surfing and Windsurfing Spots

- Birsay Bay: Known for its consistent waves, Birsay Bay is a popular spot for surfing, particularly in autumn and winter when swells are at their peak.
- Scapa Beach: A sheltered location suitable for beginners and intermediate surfers and windsurfers, offering steady winds and manageable waves.
- Bay of Skaill: Famous for its historic Skara Brae site, the Bay of Skaill also attracts surfers looking for quality waves and scenic surroundings.

Equipment Rentals and Lessons
- Orkney Surf School: Provides surfboard and wetsuit rentals, as well as lessons for beginners and intermediate surfers. Experienced instructors ensure a safe and enjoyable experience.
- Orkney Windsurfing: Offers windsurfing equipment rentals and lessons tailored to various skill levels, with a focus on safety and fun.

5. Stand-Up Paddleboarding (SUP)
Overview
Stand-up paddleboarding (SUP) is a versatile and accessible water sport that allows visitors to explore Orkney's coastline, bays, and inland waters at a leisurely pace. SUP is suitable for all ages and fitness levels.

Top SUP Locations

- Scapa Flow: The calm waters of Scapa Flow are ideal for paddleboarding, offering stunning views and opportunities to spot marine life.
- Kirkwall Bay: A safe and sheltered environment perfect for beginners and families, with easy access from the town.
- Hoy Sound: For more experienced paddleboarders, the currents and waves of Hoy Sound provide a more challenging and exhilarating experience.

SUP Rentals and Tours
- Orkney SUP: Offers paddleboard rentals, guided tours, and lessons for all skill levels. Explore hidden coves, sea caves, and pristine beaches with experienced guides.
- Kirkwall Marina: Provides SUP rentals and information on the best local spots for paddleboarding.

Safety Tips for Water Sports
- Check the Weather: Orkney's weather can change rapidly. Always check forecasts and sea conditions before heading out.
- Wear Appropriate Gear: Use a wetsuit, buoyancy aid, and other safety equipment suitable for the water temperature and conditions.
- Know Your Limits: Choose activities and locations that match your skill level. Don't hesitate

to hire a guide or take lessons if you're inexperienced.
- Respect the Environment: Follow local guidelines to protect marine life and habitats. Avoid disturbing wildlife and leave no trace.

Orkney's diverse and stunning marine environment offers a wide range of water sports adventures for visitors. Whether you're exploring hidden coves by kayak, diving among historic wrecks, sailing through scenic waters, catching waves, or paddleboarding along tranquil bays, there's something for everyone. Equip yourself with the right gear, prioritize safety, and immerse yourself in the aquatic wonders that make Orkney a top destination for water sports enthusiasts.

Historical And Archaeological Sites

Orkney is renowned for its rich history and significant archaeological sites, many of which date back thousands of years. Exploring these sites offers visitors a fascinating journey through time, revealing the ancient cultures and peoples who once inhabited these islands. Here's a comprehensive guide to some of the most important historical and archaeological sites in Orkney that outdoor enthusiasts can explore.

1. Skara Brae

Overview
- Location: Bay of Skaill, Mainland Orkney
- Dating: Neolithic period, around 3200-2200 BCE
- Highlights: Exceptionally well-preserved stone houses, detailed artifacts, and interpretive visitor center.

Site Description
Skara Brae is one of the best-preserved Neolithic settlements in Europe. Discovered in 1850, the site provides a remarkable glimpse into prehistoric life with its well-preserved stone structures, including houses complete with stone furniture. The visitor center offers insights into the daily lives of the inhabitants through displays of artifacts and interactive exhibits. The picturesque setting along the Bay of Skaill adds to the experience, making it a must-visit for history buffs and outdoor explorers alike.

2. Maeshowe

Overview
- Location: Stenness, Mainland Orkney
- Dating: Neolithic period, around 2800 BCE
- Highlights: Impressive chambered cairn, intricate Viking graffiti, and alignment with the winter solstice.

Site Description
Maeshowe is a large chambered cairn and passage grave, known for its architectural sophistication and alignment with the winter solstice. The tomb's interior features runic inscriptions left by Viking visitors in the 12th century, offering a unique blend of Neolithic and Norse history. Guided tours provide detailed explanations of the site's construction, significance, and the intriguing Viking graffiti. The surrounding landscape, part of the Heart of Neolithic Orkney UNESCO World Heritage Site, is equally captivating.

3. The Ring of Brodgar
Overview
- Location: Stenness, Mainland Orkney
- Dating: Neolithic period, around 2500-2000 BCE
- Highlights: Impressive stone circle, ceremonial landscape, and panoramic views.

Site Description
The Ring of Brodgar is an iconic stone circle and henge, originally consisting of 60 stones, with 27 still standing. It forms part of a broader ceremonial landscape that includes the Stones of Stenness and Maeshowe. The exact purpose of the circle remains a mystery, but it is believed to have been used for ritual and ceremonial purposes. The site's setting, with views over the surrounding lochs and hills,

makes it a stunning and atmospheric location for exploration.

4. The Stones of Stenness

Overview
- Location: Stenness, Mainland Orkney
- Dating: Neolithic period, around 3100 BCE
- Highlights: Tall standing stones, henge monument, and nearby Neolithic village.

Site Description
The Stones of Stenness is one of the oldest stone circles in Britain, featuring four impressive standing stones, some over 19 feet (6 meters) tall. The site originally consisted of 12 stones arranged in a circle within a henge monument. Close to the Ring of Brodgar, it forms part of the Heart of Neolithic Orkney. The nearby Barnhouse Village, a reconstructed Neolithic settlement, offers additional insights into the lives of Orkney's ancient inhabitants.

5. The Broch of Gurness

Overview
- Location: Evie, Mainland Orkney
- Dating: Iron Age, around 200-100 BCE
- Highlights: Well-preserved broch, surrounding village, and coastal views.

Site Description

The Broch of Gurness is a remarkable Iron Age settlement featuring a well-preserved broch, a type of drystone hollow-walled structure unique to Scotland. The central broch is surrounded by remains of houses and outbuildings, giving visitors a vivid impression of Iron Age life. The site overlooks Eynhallow Sound, offering beautiful coastal views and opportunities for spotting marine wildlife. Interpretive panels and reconstructions help bring the site's history to life.

6. The Tomb of the Eagles
Overview
- Location: South Ronaldsay, Orkney
- Dating: Neolithic period, around 3000 BCE
- Highlights: Chambered tomb, extensive artifacts, and interactive museum.

Site Description
Also known as Isbister Chambered Cairn, the Tomb of the Eagles is named after the large number of eagle talons found within the tomb. The site includes a chambered cairn and a Bronze Age house, offering a fascinating glimpse into prehistoric funerary practices. The adjacent visitor center displays a range of artifacts discovered at the site, including pottery, tools, and bones. Guided

tours provide detailed insights into the tomb's history and significance.

Tips for Visiting Historical and Archaeological Sites

Prepare for the Weather
- Layers: Orkney's weather can be changeable, so dress in layers to stay comfortable.
- Waterproofs: Bring waterproof clothing and sturdy footwear, especially for sites with uneven terrain.

Respect the Sites
- Leave No Trace: Follow the Leave No Trace principles to protect these ancient sites.
- Guidelines: Adhere to any guidelines or restrictions provided by site managers to preserve the integrity of the monuments.

Enhance Your Visit
- Guided Tours: Many sites offer guided tours that provide valuable context and historical background.
- Visitor Centers: Take advantage of visitor centers and museums for additional information and exhibits.

Exploring Orkney's historical and archaeological sites is an enriching outdoor adventure that connects visitors with the islands' ancient past. From the Neolithic village of Skara Brae to the imposing

Ring of Brodgar, each site offers a unique window into the lives and cultures of Orkney's early inhabitants. Whether you're a history enthusiast or simply enjoy discovering new places, Orkney's archaeological treasures promise a memorable and educational experience. Prepare for your journey, respect these ancient sites, and immerse yourself in the rich history that makes Orkney a fascinating destination.

Chapter 7

STAYING SAFE AND GREEN

Safety Tips For Travelers

Orkney is a relatively safe and welcoming destination for travelers, but like any location, it's essential to be mindful of safety practices to ensure a smooth and enjoyable trip. Here are some comprehensive safety tips for travelers to Orkney, covering a range of scenarios from outdoor activities to general precautions.

1. General Safety
Emergency Numbers
- Emergency Services: Dial 999 for police, fire, and medical emergencies.

- Non-Emergency Police: Dial 101 for non-urgent police matters.

Health Services
- NHS 24: Dial 111 for non-emergency medical advice.
- Pharmacies: Make a note of local pharmacy locations and opening hours.

2. Weather Precautions
Check the Forecast
- Daily Updates: Check local weather forecasts regularly, especially if planning outdoor activities.
- Severe Weather: Be aware of severe weather warnings and adjust plans accordingly.

Dress Appropriately
- Layers: Dress in layers to accommodate changing weather conditions.
- Waterproof Gear: Bring waterproof clothing and sturdy footwear, as Orkney can be wet and windy.

3. Outdoor Activities
Hiking and Walking
- Trail Conditions: Stick to marked trails and check for any trail conditions or closures.
- Maps and Guides: Carry a map, compass, and guidebook or app, and let someone know your route.

- Safety Equipment: Bring a first aid kit, sufficient water, snacks, and a charged mobile phone.

Wildlife Encounters
- Keep Distance: Maintain a safe distance from wildlife to avoid disturbing animals or putting yourself at risk.
- Respect Nature: Follow local guidelines to protect wildlife habitats and minimize your impact.

Water Sports
- Know Your Limits: Choose activities that match your skill level and experience.
- Safety Gear: Always wear appropriate safety gear, such as life jackets for kayaking and wetsuits for surfing.
- Guided Tours: Consider guided tours for activities like diving and kayaking to ensure safety and enhance your experience.

4. Driving and Transportation
Road Safety
- Drive on the Left: Remember that driving in Orkney is on the left side of the road.
- Speed Limits: Adhere to posted speed limits and be cautious on narrow, winding roads.
- Wildlife and Livestock: Be alert for wildlife and livestock on the roads, particularly in rural areas.

Car Rentals
- Insurance: Ensure you have comprehensive insurance coverage for your rental vehicle.
- Breakdown Services: Know the contact details for roadside assistance provided by your rental company.

5. Personal Safety
Valuables
- Secure Your Belongings: Keep your valuables secure and be mindful of your possessions in public places.
- Accommodation Security: Use the safes provided in hotels and inns to store important documents and valuables.

Solo Travel
- Stay Connected: Inform someone of your travel plans and check in regularly, especially if traveling alone.
- Trust Your Instincts: If a situation or place feels unsafe, leave immediately and seek help.

6. Health Precautions
Medications
- Bring Enough: Ensure you bring enough prescription medications for the duration of your trip, along with a copy of your prescriptions.

- Local Pharmacies: Identify local pharmacies in case you need additional supplies or over-the-counter medications.

Food and Water
- Safe Drinking Water: Tap water in Orkney is generally safe to drink, but if you have any concerns, bottled water is widely available.
- Food Hygiene: Choose reputable restaurants and cafes to ensure food safety and hygiene.

7. Environmental Awareness
Leave No Trace
- Minimize Waste: Follow the Leave No Trace principles to minimize your environmental impact.
- Recycle: Use recycling facilities provided and dispose of waste responsibly.

Cultural Respect
- Local Customs: Respect local customs and traditions, and be courteous to residents and fellow travelers.
- Historical Sites: Treat archaeological sites and historical landmarks with respect, following all posted guidelines and restrictions.

8. Technology and Connectivity
Mobile Phones

- Coverage: Mobile phone coverage is generally good, but some remote areas may have limited reception.
- Emergency Contacts: Program important emergency contacts into your phone.

Internet Access
- Wi-Fi Availability: Wi-Fi is available in most hotels, cafes, and public places. Consider bringing a portable charger for your devices.

Orkney is a beautiful and relatively safe destination for travelers, offering stunning landscapes, rich history, and a welcoming community. By following these safety tips, you can ensure a safe, enjoyable, and memorable trip. Stay informed, be prepared, and respect the local environment and customs to make the most of your Orkney adventure.

Emergency Contacts And Sevices

Ensuring you have access to emergency contacts and services is crucial for a safe and worry-free trip to Orkney. Here's a comprehensive guide to essential emergency contacts and services to help you stay prepared during your visit.

1. Emergency Numbers
General Emergency Services

- Emergency Services (Police, Fire, Ambulance): Dial 999
    - Use this number for immediate assistance in any life-threatening situation, including accidents, fires, and medical emergencies.

Non-Emergency Police
- Police Scotland (Non-Emergency): Dial 101
    - For reporting non-urgent incidents, such as minor crimes or concerns that do not require immediate emergency response.

2. **Medical Services**
NHS 24
- Non-Emergency Medical Advice: Dial 111
    - For non-emergency health concerns and medical advice, this service operates 24/7 and can provide guidance on medical issues and direct you to appropriate care.

Hospitals
- Balfour Hospital, Kirkwall
    - Address: New Scapa Road, Kirkwall, Orkney KW15 1BH
    - Phone: +44 1856 888000
    - Provides comprehensive medical services, including an accident and emergency department.

Pharmacies

- Boots Pharmacy, Kirkwall
  - Address: 13 Albert Street, Kirkwall, Orkney KW15 1HP
  - Phone: +44 1856 872059

- Sutherlands Pharmacy, Stromness
  - Address: 91 Victoria Street, Stromness, Orkney KW16 3BS
  - Phone: +44 1856 850484

3. Coastguard Services

Maritime and Coastguard Agency
- Emergency Coastguard: Dial 999 and ask for the Coastguard
  - For any emergencies at sea or along the coast, including accidents, stranded vessels, and individuals in distress.

Local Coastguard Stations
- Kirkwall Coastguard Rescue Team
  - Provides rescue and response services for coastal emergencies.

4. Breakdown and Recovery Services

AA (Automobile Association)
- Roadside Assistance: Dial +44 800 88 77 66
  - Provides breakdown recovery services and roadside assistance for vehicle issues.

RAC (Royal Automobile Club)
- Roadside Assistance: Dial +44 330 159 1111
  - Offers comprehensive breakdown cover and recovery services.

5. Tourist Information and Support
VisitScotland Information Centre, Kirkwall
- Address: 2 West Castle Street, Kirkwall, Orkney KW15 1GU
- Phone: +44 1856 872856
- Services: Provides travel advice, maps, accommodation booking assistance, and local information.

Orkney Islands Council
- Address: School Place, Kirkwall, Orkney KW15 1NY
- Phone: +44 1856 873535
- Website: [Orkney Islands Council](https://www.orkney.gov.uk/)
- Services: Offers information on local services, public transportation, and community resources.

6. Embassy and Consulate Contacts
Nearest Embassy/Consulate
- United States Consulate General Edinburgh
  - Address: 3 Regent Terrace, Edinburgh EH7 5BW
  - Phone: +44 131 556 8315

- Provides assistance to US citizens, including passport services, emergency assistance, and notarial services.

- Canadian High Commission in London
  - Address: Canada House, Trafalgar Square, London SW1Y 5BJ
  - Phone: +44 207 004 6000
  - Offers services to Canadian citizens, including emergency assistance and consular services.

7. Local Services
Local Authorities and Utilities
- Orkney Islands Council Emergency Out of Hours: Dial +44 1856 888000
- For emergencies involving public utilities, housing issues, or other council services outside of normal working hours.

Animal Control
- Orkney Islands Council Environmental Health (Animal Welfare): Dial +44 1856 873535 ext. 2901
- For concerns regarding animal welfare or stray animals.

8. Travel Insurance and Assistance
Travel Insurance Providers
- Ensure you have comprehensive travel insurance that covers medical emergencies, trip cancellations,

and other potential issues. Keep your insurance provider's contact information handy.

9. Safety Apps and Online Resources

Smartphone Apps
- What3Words: Provides precise locations using a unique combination of three words, useful for emergency services.
- Red Cross First Aid: Offers first aid advice and emergency response tips.
- NHS App: For accessing health services, booking appointments, and getting medical advice.

Online Resources
- VisitOrkney.com: Offers up-to-date travel information, local news, and safety advice.
- Orkney Islands Council Website: Provides details on local services, emergency contacts, and community alerts.

Being prepared with the right emergency contacts and knowledge of available services can make a significant difference in ensuring your safety while visiting Orkney. Keep this guide handy, familiarize yourself with local emergency procedures, and enjoy a worry-free adventure in this beautiful archipelago.

Eco-friendly Travel Practices

Traveling to Orkney offers an opportunity to explore stunning natural landscapes, rich wildlife, and historic sites. Practicing eco-friendly travel ensures that these precious resources are preserved for future generations. Here's a comprehensive guide to eco-friendly travel practices for your visit to Orkney.

1. Sustainable Transportation
Public Transport
- Buses: Utilize Orkney's bus services operated by Stagecoach, which cover key locations across the islands. Buses are a more sustainable option than driving individual cars.
- Ferries: Take advantage of Orkney Ferries for island hopping. Ferries are an essential and eco-friendly mode of transport within the archipelago.
- Cycling: Rent bicycles to explore the islands. Orkney's relatively flat terrain makes it ideal for cycling, which reduces your carbon footprint and allows you to experience the landscape more intimately.
- Walking: Embrace walking as a mode of transportation, especially in towns and villages. Walking is the greenest way to travel and lets you discover hidden gems.

2. Eco-Friendly Accommodation

Sustainable Hotels and Inns
- Green Practices: Choose accommodations that prioritize sustainable practices, such as energy-efficient lighting, water-saving fixtures, and waste reduction programs.
- Local Ownership: Support locally-owned accommodations that contribute to the local economy and often implement environmentally friendly policies.

Bed and Breakfasts
- Local Ingredients: Opt for B&Bs that use locally sourced and organic ingredients for their meals.
- Minimal Waste: Select B&Bs that have a clear commitment to reducing waste, such as offering bulk toiletries instead of single-use plastics.

Camping and Glamping
- Leave No Trace: Practice the Leave No Trace principles by minimizing your impact on the natural environment, packing out all waste, and avoiding damage to vegetation.
- Eco-Friendly Sites: Choose campsites and glamping locations that implement sustainable practices, such as renewable energy use and waste recycling.

3. Responsible Wildlife Watching
Keep a Safe Distance

- Observe Respectfully: Maintain a respectful distance from wildlife to avoid disturbing their natural behaviors.
- Use Binoculars: Bring binoculars for birdwatching and observing marine life, ensuring you can enjoy wildlife without getting too close.

Follow Guidelines
- Guided Tours: Participate in guided wildlife tours that follow ethical guidelines and respect wildlife habitats.
- No Feeding: Do not feed wildlife, as human food can harm animals and disrupt their natural diet and behavior.

4. Reducing Waste
Reusable Items
- Water Bottles: Bring a reusable water bottle to avoid single-use plastics. Tap water in Orkney is safe to drink.
- Shopping Bags: Use reusable shopping bags when purchasing souvenirs or groceries.
- Utensils and Containers: Carry reusable utensils, straws, and containers for takeout meals and snacks.

Proper Disposal
- Recycle: Use recycling bins provided in towns and accommodations for paper, glass, and plastic waste.

- Compost: If possible, compost organic waste or inquire if your accommodation has composting facilities.

5. Supporting Local and Sustainable Businesses
Local Products
- Souvenirs: Buy souvenirs made by local artisans using sustainable materials. Look for products like Orkney wool, crafts, and local artwork.
- Food and Drink: Dine at restaurants that source their ingredients locally and support sustainable fishing and farming practices.

Ethical Tours
- Certified Operators: Choose tour operators that are certified for their sustainable practices and commitment to eco-friendly tourism.
- Small Groups: Opt for tours with small group sizes to minimize environmental impact and enhance your experience.

6. Conserving Natural Resources
Water Conservation
- Short Showers: Take shorter showers to conserve water, especially in accommodations with limited water resources.
- Mindful Usage: Be mindful of water use when brushing teeth, washing dishes, and using water for other activities.

Energy Efficiency
- Switch Off: Turn off lights, heating, and electronic devices when not in use.
- Energy-Saving Settings: Use energy-saving settings on electronic devices and appliances.

7. Cultural Respect and Education
Learn and Share
- Local Customs: Learn about and respect local customs, traditions, and cultural practices.
- Educational Tours: Participate in educational tours and activities that teach about Orkney's natural and cultural heritage.

Volunteer Opportunities
- Eco-Volunteering: Consider participating in eco-volunteering projects, such as beach clean-ups or conservation work, to give back to the community and environment.

8. Minimal Impact Exploration
Stay on Trails
- Marked Paths: Stick to marked trails and paths to protect natural habitats and prevent soil erosion.
- Respect Closures: Respect any trail or area closures designed to protect sensitive ecosystems.

Leave What You Find

- Natural and Cultural Artifacts: Do not take rocks, plants, or cultural artifacts as souvenirs. Leave natural and historical sites undisturbed for others to enjoy.

Practicing eco-friendly travel in Orkney helps preserve its unique natural beauty and rich heritage. By adopting sustainable transportation, choosing green accommodations, reducing waste, supporting local businesses, and conserving resources, you can enjoy a memorable and responsible visit to Orkney. Embrace these eco-friendly practices to ensure that future generations can also experience the magic of these islands.

Conservation And Responsible Tourism

Orkney's pristine landscapes, rich wildlife, and historical sites make it a unique destination that deserves careful conservation and responsible tourism practices. By prioritizing sustainability, visitors can help preserve Orkney's natural and cultural heritage for future generations. Here's a comprehensive guide on how to practice conservation and responsible tourism while exploring Orkney.

1. Understanding Conservation in Orkney
Protecting Natural Habitats

- Wildlife Reserves: Orkney is home to several wildlife reserves, such as the RSPB Scotland reserves, which protect important bird habitats.
- Marine Conservation: Orkney's waters are part of marine conservation areas that safeguard marine life and ecosystems.

Historical and Archaeological Preservation
- World Heritage Sites: Orkney's Heart of Neolithic Orkney is a UNESCO World Heritage Site, including Skara Brae, Maeshowe, and the Ring of Brodgar.
- Ongoing Research: Archaeological sites are actively researched and conserved to ensure their preservation and understanding.

2. Responsible Tourism Practices
Minimize Environmental Impact
- Eco-Friendly Transport: Use sustainable transportation options like walking, cycling, public buses, and ferries to reduce carbon emissions.
- Waste Reduction: Avoid single-use plastics, recycle where possible, and properly dispose of all waste.

Respecting Wildlife
- Safe Distances: Observe wildlife from a distance to avoid disturbing their natural behaviors.

- No Feeding: Do not feed wild animals, as it can harm their health and alter their natural behaviors.

3. Supporting Local Communities
Buy Local
- Local Products: Purchase locally made crafts, food, and souvenirs to support the Orkney economy and reduce the environmental impact of imported goods.
- Farmers' Markets: Visit farmers' markets to buy fresh, local produce directly from the producers.

Ethical Tourism Operators
- Certified Providers: Choose tour operators and guides certified for their sustainable practices.
- Small Group Tours: Opt for small group tours to minimize environmental impact and foster a more personalized experience.

4. Sustainable Accommodation
Green Hotels and B&Bs
- Energy Efficiency: Stay at accommodations that use renewable energy sources and implement energy-saving measures.
- Water Conservation: Choose places that practice water conservation and offer guests ways to participate.

Eco-Friendly Camping

- Leave No Trace: Follow the Leave No Trace principles by packing out all waste, minimizing campfire impacts, and respecting wildlife.
- Certified Sites: Use campsites certified for their eco-friendly practices.

5. Participating in Conservation Efforts
Volunteering
- Conservation Projects: Join local conservation projects, such as beach clean-ups, wildlife monitoring, or habitat restoration.
- Community Initiatives: Engage with community-led sustainability initiatives and learn how you can contribute.

Education and Advocacy
- Local Knowledge: Learn about Orkney's conservation efforts through museums, visitor centers, and guided tours.
- Spread Awareness: Share your knowledge and experiences about Orkney's conservation efforts to raise awareness and promote responsible tourism.

6. Engaging with Local Culture
Cultural Respect
- Local Customs: Respect local traditions, languages, and practices. Engage with locals to learn more about their culture and history.

- Archaeological Sites: Follow guidelines at historical and archaeological sites to avoid damaging these precious resources.

Sustainable Events
- Eco-Friendly Festivals: Participate in local festivals and events that prioritize sustainability and cultural heritage.
- Cultural Workshops: Attend workshops and activities that promote traditional crafts, music, and practices.

7. Responsible Outdoor Activities
Hiking and Walking
- Marked Trails: Stick to designated trails to protect natural habitats and prevent soil erosion.
- Leave No Trace: Carry out all litter, avoid picking plants, and leave the environment as you found it.

Water Activities
- Eco-Friendly Practices: Choose water sports operators who practice environmentally friendly methods and adhere to conservation guidelines.
- Marine Protection: Follow guidelines to protect marine life, such as avoiding touching coral and not disturbing marine animals.

8. Planning and Preparation
Research and Planning

- Learn Before You Go: Research Orkney's natural and cultural heritage before your visit to understand the importance of conservation.
- Sustainable Travel Plans: Plan your trip with sustainability in mind, considering the environmental impact of your activities and choices.

Travel Insurance
- Eco-Coverage: Ensure your travel insurance includes coverage for eco-friendly and responsible tourism activities.

Conservation and responsible tourism in Orkney involve making thoughtful choices that respect and protect the natural environment and cultural heritage. By following sustainable practices, supporting local communities, and engaging in conservation efforts, you can contribute to preserving Orkney's unique beauty and history. Enjoy your visit responsibly, ensuring that Orkney remains a remarkable destination for generations to come.

Chapter 8

ESSENTIAL PLANNING

When To Visit

Choosing the best time to visit Orkney can enhance your experience, whether you're interested in outdoor adventures, cultural events, or simply enjoying the scenic beauty of the islands. Here's a comprehensive guide on when to visit Orkney, highlighting seasonal attractions, weather conditions, and key events throughout the year.

Spring (March to May)
Weather
- Temperature: Average highs range from 7°C (45°F) in March to 12°C (54°F) in May.

- Conditions: Spring brings longer days, milder temperatures, and blooming wildflowers.

Attractions and Activities
- Bird Watching: Spring is ideal for birdwatching as migratory birds return to the islands. RSPB reserves like Marwick Head and The Loons are excellent spots.
- Wildflowers: The countryside comes alive with blooming wildflowers, perfect for hiking and photography.
- Lambing Season: Witness the adorable sight of newborn lambs in the fields.

Events
- Orkney Nature Festival: Celebrating Orkney's natural heritage with guided walks, boat trips, and wildlife watching.

Summer (June to August)
Weather
- Temperature: Average highs range from 14°C (57°F) in June to 16°C (61°F) in August.
- Conditions: Summer offers the warmest weather, long daylight hours, and relatively low rainfall.

Attractions and Activities
- Outdoor Adventures: Ideal for hiking, cycling, and water sports. Explore trails, cliffs, and beaches.

- Festivals: Summer is festival season in Orkney, with various cultural and music events.
- Historical Sites: Visit Neolithic sites like Skara Brae, Maeshowe, and the Ring of Brodgar in pleasant weather.

Events
- St Magnus International Festival: A celebration of arts and culture, featuring music, theater, and dance.
- Orkney Folk Festival: A lively event showcasing traditional music and dance.
- Shows and Agricultural Fairs: Local events celebrating Orkney's agricultural heritage with livestock displays, crafts, and food.

Autumn (September to November)
Weather
- Temperature: Average highs range from 14°C (57°F) in September to 9°C (48°F) in November.
- Conditions: Autumn brings cooler temperatures, shorter days, and the stunning colors of changing foliage.

Attractions and Activities
- Wildlife Watching: Autumn is excellent for spotting seals and their pups, as well as migratory birds preparing for winter.
- Scenic Walks: Enjoy walks in the crisp autumn air with beautiful landscapes and fewer tourists.

- Harvest Season: Experience the local harvest, with fresh produce and traditional foods.

Events
- Orkney Science Festival: Engaging talks, workshops, and exhibitions celebrating science and innovation.
- Orkney Blues Festival: A vibrant event featuring live blues music performances across various venues.

Winter (December to February)
Weather
- Temperature: Average highs range from 7°C (45°F) in December to 6°C (43°F) in February.
- Conditions: Winter is characterized by short days, cool temperatures, and occasional storms. However, the scenery can be dramatic and beautiful.

Attractions and Activities
- Northern Lights: Winter offers the chance to witness the Aurora Borealis (Northern Lights) on clear nights.
- Festive Celebrations: Experience traditional Scottish celebrations during the festive season, including Christmas and Hogmanay.
- Quiet Exploration: Enjoy a peaceful visit with fewer tourists, perfect for those seeking solitude and reflection.

Events
- Hogmanay: Celebrate the New Year with traditional Scottish festivities, music, and fireworks.
- Up Helly Aa: A Viking-themed fire festival held in January in nearby Shetland, which can be combined with a trip to Orkney.

Special Considerations
School Holidays and Peak Seasons
- Peak Tourist Season: June to August is the busiest time, so book accommodations and activities in advance.
- School Holidays: Be aware of UK school holidays (mid-July to early September), as these can affect availability and prices.

Wildlife Timing
- Bird Migration: Spring and autumn are peak times for birdwatching due to migratory patterns.
- Seal Pups: Autumn is the best time to see seal pups along the coast.

Weather-Dependent Activities
- Outdoor Sports: Plan water sports, hiking, and cycling for spring to autumn when the weather is more favorable.

- Winter Attractions: Be prepared for limited daylight and variable weather in winter, affecting some outdoor activities.

Orkney offers unique experiences year-round, from vibrant summer festivals and wildlife watching to peaceful winter landscapes and cultural events. By considering the seasonal weather, attractions, and events, you can plan your visit to Orkney for the optimal experience based on your interests and preferences. Whether you seek adventure, culture, or tranquility, Orkney has something to offer in every season.

Packing List

Packing appropriately for a trip to Orkney is crucial to ensure you have a comfortable and enjoyable experience, regardless of the season. The weather can be variable, and the activities diverse, so here's a comprehensive packing list to help you prepare for your visit.

1. Clothing
Layering Essentials
- Base Layers: Moisture-wicking base layers (tops and bottoms) for warmth and comfort.
- Mid Layers: Fleece or wool sweaters for insulation.

- Outer Layers: Waterproof and windproof jacket and trousers for protection against rain and wind.

Seasonal Items
- Spring and Summer: Lightweight clothing, such as t-shirts, shorts, and lightweight trousers. Include a warm sweater or jacket for cooler evenings.
- Autumn and Winter: Thermal layers, insulated jacket, hat, gloves, and scarves to stay warm in colder temperatures.

Footwear
- Hiking Boots: Sturdy, waterproof hiking boots for exploring trails and rugged terrain.
- Comfortable Shoes: For walking around towns and villages.
- Sandals: Optional for warmer days in summer.

Accessories
- Hats: Sun hat for summer and a warm hat for winter.
- Gloves and Scarves: Essential in autumn and winter.
- Socks: Warm, moisture-wicking socks for hiking and daily wear.
- Swimwear: If you plan to enjoy water sports or visit indoor pools.

2. Outdoor Gear

Daypack
- Backpack: A comfortable daypack for carrying essentials during excursions.

Hiking Gear
- Walking Poles: Optional but useful for uneven terrain.
- Water Bottle: Reusable and durable water bottle.
- Snacks: Energy bars, nuts, and dried fruits for hikes and outdoor activities.
- Map and Compass: Even if you use GPS, having a physical map and compass can be helpful.

Water Sports Gear
- Wetsuit: If you plan on participating in water sports, such as surfing or kayaking.
- Towel: Quick-dry towel for water activities.

3. Technology and Gadgets
Communication
- Mobile Phone: With a charger and portable power bank.
- Travel Adapter: UK plug adapter if your devices use a different type of plug.

Photography
- Camera: With extra batteries and memory cards.
- Binoculars: For bird watching and wildlife spotting.

Navigation and Safety
- GPS Device: Handy for navigation during hikes and remote explorations.
- Headlamp or Flashlight: Useful for low-light conditions and emergencies.

4. Personal Items

Documents
- Passport/ID: Ensure it is valid and not expiring soon.
- Travel Insurance: Documentation for travel insurance covering medical emergencies and trip cancellations.
- Tickets and Reservations: Printed or digital copies of your travel tickets, accommodation bookings, and activity reservations.

Health and Hygiene
- Medications: Any prescription medications you require, plus a small first-aid kit with basics like band-aids, antiseptic wipes, and pain relievers.
- Toiletries: Travel-sized toiletries including toothbrush, toothpaste, shampoo, conditioner, soap, and deodorant.
- Sun Protection: Sunscreen, lip balm with SPF, and sunglasses.

5. Travel Comfort

In-Flight or In-Transit
- Travel Pillow: For comfort during flights or ferry rides.
- Eye Mask and Earplugs: For better rest during travel.
- Entertainment: Books, magazines, or e-readers for downtime.

6. Miscellaneous
Reusable Items
- Reusable Bags: For shopping and carrying extra items.
- Reusable Cutlery and Containers: For picnics or takeaway meals.

Local Currency
- Cash and Cards: Bring a mix of cash (British Pounds) and cards. While cards are widely accepted, some small businesses may prefer cash.

Emergency Contact Information
- Important Contacts: A list of emergency contacts, including local emergency numbers and contact details for your accommodation.

Packing thoughtfully for Orkney ensures that you're prepared for its diverse weather and activities. Focus on layering your clothing, bringing essential outdoor gear, and including personal and travel items for comfort and safety. By following this comprehensive packing list, you'll be well-equipped to enjoy everything Orkney has to offer.

Health And Travel Insurance

Traveling to Orkney requires thorough preparation, including ensuring your health and travel insurance needs are covered. Proper insurance can provide peace of mind and protection against unexpected events. Here's a comprehensive guide on what you need to know about health and travel insurance for your trip to Orkney.

1. Health Insurance
European Health Insurance Card (EHIC) / Global Health Insurance Card (GHIC)
- UK and EU Citizens: If you're a citizen of the UK or EU, make sure you have an EHIC or GHIC. These cards provide access to state-provided healthcare in Orkney at a reduced cost or sometimes for free.
- Validity: Check the expiration date on your card and renew it if necessary before your trip.

International Travelers
- Health Insurance: Non-EU/UK travelers should ensure their health insurance policy covers medical treatment abroad, including in the UK.

- Coverage: Confirm that your policy includes coverage for doctor visits, hospital stays, emergency services, and prescription medications.

2. Travel Insurance
Comprehensive Travel Insurance
- Policy Coverage: Opt for comprehensive travel insurance that includes coverage for trip cancellations, delays, lost or stolen baggage, and medical emergencies.
- Medical Coverage: Ensure the policy covers emergency medical expenses, including hospital stays, treatments, and medical evacuation if necessary.

Special Considerations
- Adventure Activities: If you plan to engage in adventure activities like hiking, cycling, or water sports, make sure your insurance policy covers these activities.
- Pre-Existing Conditions: Declare any pre-existing medical conditions to your insurer to ensure they are covered.

3. Types of Travel Insurance
Single Trip Insurance
- Duration: Covers one trip for a specific period.
- Benefits: Ideal for short-term visitors who do not plan to travel frequently within the policy period.

Annual Multi-Trip Insurance
- Duration: Covers multiple trips within a year.
- Benefits: Cost-effective for frequent travelers who plan to visit Orkney or other destinations multiple times in a year.

4. Key Elements of a Good Travel Insurance Policy

Medical Emergency and Evacuation
- Emergency Care: Coverage for medical emergencies, including hospital stays, surgeries, and doctor visits.
- Evacuation: Coverage for medical evacuation to the nearest appropriate medical facility or back home if necessary.

Trip Cancellation and Interruption
- Cancellation: Reimbursement for prepaid, non-refundable expenses if you need to cancel your trip due to covered reasons such as illness, injury, or unforeseen events.
- Interruption: Coverage for additional expenses if your trip is interrupted and you need to return home earlier than planned.

Baggage and Personal Belongings

- Lost/Stolen Baggage: Compensation for lost, stolen, or damaged baggage and personal belongings.
- Delayed Baggage: Reimbursement for essential items if your baggage is delayed for a certain period.

Travel Delays
- Accommodation and Meals: Coverage for additional accommodation and meal expenses incurred due to travel delays.

5. Emergency Assistance Services
24/7 Support
- Helpline: Ensure your insurance policy includes 24/7 emergency assistance services.
- Support: Access to support for medical emergencies, travel issues, and other urgent situations.

6. How to Choose the Right Insurance Policy
Compare Policies
- Research: Compare different insurance policies and providers to find one that offers the best coverage for your needs.
- Read Reviews: Look for customer reviews and ratings to assess the reliability and quality of service of the insurance provider.

Understand Exclusions
- Policy Exclusions: Carefully read the policy documents to understand any exclusions or limitations, such as activities not covered or specific health conditions.
- Fine Print: Pay attention to the fine print and ask the insurer for clarification if needed.

7. Practical Tips
Documentation
- Carry Copies: Carry physical and digital copies of your insurance policy, EHIC/GHIC card, and emergency contact information.
- Emergency Numbers: Note down the emergency contact numbers provided by your insurance company.

Pre-Travel Health Check
- Consult Your Doctor: Visit your doctor for a health check-up before traveling to Orkney, especially if you have existing medical conditions.
- Medications: Ensure you have enough supply of any prescription medications you need, along with a copy of the prescription.

8. In Case of Emergency
Contact Your Insurer

- Immediate Notification: Contact your insurance provider as soon as possible in case of a medical emergency or any other covered incident.
- Documentation: Keep all receipts, medical reports, and other relevant documentation to support your insurance claim.

Proper health and travel insurance are essential components of planning a trip to Orkney. By ensuring comprehensive coverage for medical emergencies, travel disruptions, and personal belongings, you can travel with peace of mind, knowing you are protected against unexpected events. Take the time to choose the right insurance policy, understand its terms and conditions, and carry the necessary documentation to ensure a safe and enjoyable visit to Orkney.

Visa And Entry Requirements

Traveling to Orkney involves understanding the visa and entry requirements based on your nationality and the purpose of your visit. Here's a detailed guide to help you navigate the visa process and ensure a smooth entry into Orkney.

1. Visa Requirements
European Union (EU) and European Economic Area (EEA) Citizens

- Visa-Free Travel: EU and EEA citizens do not need a visa to enter the UK, including Orkney, for short stays up to 6 months.
- Passport/ID: A valid passport or national ID card is required for entry.

Non-EU/EEA Citizens
- Visa Types: Depending on your nationality, you may need a visa to enter the UK. Common visa types include tourist visas, business visas, and student visas.
- Visa Waiver Program: Citizens of certain countries, such as the USA, Canada, Australia, and Japan, can enter the UK for short stays up to 6 months without a visa under the Visa Waiver Program. Check the UK government website for the full list of eligible countries.

Common Visa Categories
- Standard Visitor Visa: For tourism, short business trips, and family visits. Valid for up to 6 months.
- Short-Term Study Visa: For short-term courses (up to 6 months).
- Work Visa: Required for those planning to work in the UK. Types include the Skilled Worker Visa and Temporary Worker Visa.

2. How to Apply for a Visa
Online Application

- UK Government Website: Visit the UK Visas and Immigration (UKVI) website to start your visa application process.
- Application Form: Complete the online visa application form, providing accurate and detailed information.

Required Documents
- Passport: A valid passport with at least six months remaining validity.
- Photographs: Recent passport-sized photographs meeting UKVI specifications.
- Proof of Funds: Bank statements or financial documents showing you have enough money to support yourself during your stay.
- Travel Itinerary: Details of your planned activities in Orkney, including accommodation and transportation bookings.
- Supporting Documents: Additional documents depending on the visa type (e.g., invitation letter for a business visa, enrollment confirmation for a student visa).

Visa Fees
- Payment: Pay the visa application fee online during the application process. Fees vary depending on the visa type and duration of stay.

Biometrics Appointment

- Biometrics: Schedule an appointment at a visa application center to provide biometric information (fingerprints and photograph).

3. Entry Requirements
Border Control
- Passport Check: Present your passport and visa (if applicable) to the Border Force officer at the UK port of entry.
- Questions: Be prepared to answer questions about your visit, including your accommodation, travel plans, and financial means.

Additional Documentation
- Return Ticket: Proof of a return or onward travel ticket.
- Accommodation Details: Confirmation of your accommodation arrangements in Orkney.
- Travel Insurance: Proof of valid travel insurance covering your stay in the UK.

4. Customs Regulations
Restricted and Prohibited Items
- Items to Declare: Certain goods, such as large sums of cash (over £10,000), food items, and plant materials, must be declared at customs.
- Prohibited Items: Items such as illegal drugs, offensive weapons, and certain animal products are prohibited and should not be brought into the UK.

Duty-Free Allowances
- Limits: Be aware of duty-free allowances for bringing in goods such as alcohol, tobacco, and gifts. Check the HM Revenue and Customs (HMRC) website for current limits.

5. Special Considerations
Traveling with Children
- Consent Letters: If traveling with children who are not your own, carry a consent letter from the child's parents or legal guardians.
- Child's Documentation: Ensure children have their own passports and any necessary visas.

6. Staying Compliant
Duration of Stay
- Stay Limits: Adhere to the allowed duration of stay as specified by your visa type. Overstaying can result in penalties and future visa application issues.
- Extension: If you need to extend your stay, apply for a visa extension through the UKVI before your current visa expires.

7. Practical Tips
Plan Ahead
- Early Application: Apply for your visa well in advance of your planned travel dates to allow for processing time.

- Document Copies: Keep copies of all your travel documents, visa, and insurance details.

Contact Information
- Embassy/Consulate: Note the contact details of your country's embassy or consulate in the UK for assistance if needed.

Understanding and adhering to visa and entry requirements is crucial for a hassle-free visit to Orkney. Whether you're traveling from within the EU, EEA, or beyond, ensure you have the correct visa, required documents, and knowledge of entry procedures. Proper planning and preparation will help you enjoy your Orkney adventure with peace of mind, knowing all legal and procedural aspects are covered.

Chapter 9

SAMPLED ITINERARY

Weekend Getaway

A weekend getaway to Orkney offers a perfect blend of historical exploration, scenic beauty, and local culture. Here's a detailed itinerary to help you make the most of your short trip to this enchanting archipelago.

Day 1: Arrival and Initial Exploration
Morning: Arrival in Orkney
- Travel to Orkney: Arrive in Orkney via flight to Kirkwall Airport or ferry to Stromness.
- Check-In: Settle into your accommodation in Kirkwall or Stromness.

Late Morning: Exploring Kirkwall

- St. Magnus Cathedral: Start your journey with a visit to St. Magnus Cathedral, a stunning example of medieval architecture and a prominent landmark in Kirkwall.
- Orkney Museum: Explore the Orkney Museum to learn about the islands' history, from prehistoric times to the Viking era.

Lunch: Local Cuisine in Kirkwall
- Lunch Spot: Enjoy a delicious lunch at a local café or restaurant, such as The Reel or The Bothy, to sample Orkney's fresh seafood and local produce.

Afternoon: Historical Sites
- Earl's Palace: Visit the ruins of the Earl's Palace, a striking Renaissance structure near the cathedral.
- Bishop's Palace: Explore the nearby Bishop's Palace, another historic site offering insights into Orkney's medieval past.

Late Afternoon: Scapa Flow
- Scapa Flow: Take a short drive to Scapa Flow, a natural harbor with significant wartime history. Visit the Scapa Flow Visitor Centre and Museum to learn about its role in both World Wars.

Evening: Dinner and Local Culture

- Dinner: Dine at a recommended restaurant like Helgi's or The Foveran, enjoying traditional Orkney dishes.
- Local Pubs: Experience Orkney's local culture with a visit to a traditional pub. Try The Orkney Brewery or The Auld Motor Hoose for local brews and lively atmosphere.

Day 2: Neolithic Orkney and Coastal Beauty
Morning: Neolithic Heartland
- Skara Brae: Start your day early with a visit to Skara Brae, a remarkably well-preserved Neolithic village. Explore the ancient dwellings and the nearby Skaill House.
- Ring of Brodgar: Next, head to the Ring of Brodgar, a dramatic stone circle dating back to the Neolithic period. Walk around the site and take in the mystical atmosphere.
- Standing Stones of Stenness: Close to the Ring of Brodgar, visit the Standing Stones of Stenness, another significant prehistoric site.

Lunch: Countryside Picnic
- Picnic: Pack a picnic lunch or grab a takeaway from a local deli to enjoy amidst the stunning countryside or by the shores of a nearby loch.

Afternoon: Coastal Exploration

- Yesnaby Cliffs: Drive to Yesnaby Cliffs for a breathtaking coastal walk. The dramatic cliffs, sea stacks, and views of the Atlantic Ocean make for fantastic photo opportunities.
- Brough of Birsay: If the tide permits, visit the Brough of Birsay, an island accessible by a causeway. Explore the remains of a Norse settlement and enjoy panoramic views.

Late Afternoon: Relaxation and Shopping
- Local Shops: Return to Kirkwall or Stromness for some leisurely shopping. Explore local craft shops, art galleries, and boutiques for unique Orkney souvenirs.
- Tea and Treats: Stop by a local café for tea and Orkney delicacies like bere bannocks or Orkney fudge.

Evening: Farewell Dinner and Sunset
- Dinner: Choose a cozy restaurant for a farewell dinner. Consider dining at The Bayleaf Delicatessen or The Ferry Inn for a memorable meal.
- Sunset Viewing: End your day by watching the sunset from a scenic spot such as the cliffs at Yesnaby or a peaceful beach like Waulkmill Bay.

Day 3: Departure and Final Exploration
Morning: Final Exploration

- Italian Chapel: On your way to the airport or ferry terminal, visit the Italian Chapel on Lamb Holm. This beautifully decorated chapel was built by Italian POWs during WWII and is a testament to hope and creativity.
- Churchill Barriers: Drive across the Churchill Barriers, built during WWII, and stop to explore the wrecks and scenic views along the way.

Late Morning: Departure
- Check-Out: Check out of your accommodation and make your way to the airport or ferry terminal.
- Last-Minute Shopping: If time allows, do some last-minute shopping for Orkney produce, crafts, and souvenirs at local shops or the airport/ferry terminal.

Practical Tips
- Accommodation: Book accommodations in advance, especially during peak seasons. Consider staying in a central location like Kirkwall or Stromness for convenience.
- Transport: Renting a car is recommended for easy access to various sites. Alternatively, use local buses and taxis.
- Weather: Be prepared for changing weather. Pack layers, waterproof clothing, and sturdy footwear for outdoor activities.

- Local Etiquette: Respect local customs and natural sites. Take care to leave no trace when exploring the outdoors.

A weekend in Orkney offers a perfect blend of history, culture, and natural beauty. By following this itinerary, you'll experience the best of Orkney's attractions, from ancient Neolithic sites to stunning coastal landscapes, ensuring a memorable and enriching getaway.

5-Day Adventure

Orkney is a treasure trove of history, nature, and adventure. This 5-day itinerary will help you explore the islands thoroughly, providing a perfect balance of sightseeing, outdoor activities, and local experiences.

Day 1: Arrival and Exploring Kirkwall
Morning: Arrival in Orkney
- Travel to Orkney: Arrive via flight to Kirkwall Airport or ferry to Stromness.
- Check-In: Settle into your accommodation in Kirkwall.

Late Morning: Discovering Kirkwall

- St. Magnus Cathedral: Begin with a visit to the iconic St. Magnus Cathedral, a magnificent example of medieval architecture.
- Orkney Museum: Learn about Orkney's rich history at the Orkney Museum, located nearby.

Lunch: Local Cuisine
- Lunch Spot: Enjoy a meal at a local café or restaurant such as The Reel or The Bothy.

Afternoon: Historical Sites
- Earl's Palace and Bishop's Palace: Explore the ruins of the Earl's Palace and the adjacent Bishop's Palace, both showcasing impressive Renaissance architecture.

Evening: Local Culture
- Dinner: Dine at a traditional restaurant like Helgi's or The Foveran.
- Local Pubs: Experience Orkney's nightlife at a local pub such as The Orkney Brewery or The Auld Motor Hoose.

Day 2: Neolithic Orkney and Coastal Exploration
Morning: Neolithic Heartland
- Skara Brae: Visit the well-preserved Neolithic village of Skara Brae and the nearby Skaill House.

- Ring of Brodgar: Explore the Ring of Brodgar, a dramatic stone circle.
- Standing Stones of Stenness: Visit the nearby Standing Stones of Stenness.

Lunch: Countryside Picnic
- Picnic: Enjoy a picnic lunch amidst the beautiful countryside or by the shore of a loch.

Afternoon: Coastal Beauty
- Yesnaby Cliffs: Walk along the stunning Yesnaby Cliffs, known for their dramatic sea stacks and Atlantic views.

Evening: Return to Kirkwall
- Dinner: Return to Kirkwall for dinner at a recommended restaurant.
- Relax: Relax and prepare for the next day's adventures.

Day 3: Island Hopping and Outdoor Adventures
Morning: Rousay Island
- Ferry to Rousay: Take a morning ferry to Rousay, known as the "Egypt of the North" for its archaeological sites.
- Taversoe Tuick and Midhowe Cairn: Visit these ancient burial sites and enjoy the island's natural beauty.

Lunch: Local Delights
- Rousay Lunch: Have lunch at a local café or enjoy a packed lunch by the coast.

Afternoon: Exploring Rousay
- Walks and Wildlife: Explore Rousay's walking trails and look out for local wildlife, including seals and seabirds.

Evening: Return to Mainland Orkney
- Ferry Back: Return to Mainland Orkney and have dinner in Kirkwall or Stromness.

Day 4: Outdoor Adventures and Scenic Drives
Morning: Brough of Birsay
- Visit Brough of Birsay: Cross the tidal causeway (check tide times) to explore the island's ruins and lighthouse.

Late Morning: Eynhallow Sound
- Wildlife Watching: Take a boat trip around Eynhallow Sound for excellent wildlife viewing, including puffins, seals, and possibly whales.

Lunch: Coastal Café
- Lunch Spot: Enjoy a meal at a coastal café such as the Birsay Bay Tearoom.

Afternoon: Scapa Flow

- Scapa Flow: Visit Scapa Flow Visitor Centre and Museum to learn about Orkney's wartime history.

Evening: Sunset at a Scenic Spot
- Dinner: Have dinner in Kirkwall or Stromness.
- Sunset Viewing: Watch the sunset from a scenic location such as Yesnaby Cliffs or Waulkmill Bay.

Day 5: Final Exploration and Departure
Morning: South Ronaldsay
- Italian Chapel: Visit the beautifully decorated Italian Chapel on Lamb Holm.
- Churchill Barriers: Drive across the Churchill Barriers and explore the scenic spots and wrecks.

Late Morning: St. Margaret's Hope
- St. Margaret's Hope: Explore this charming village, visit local shops, and enjoy the tranquil atmosphere.

Lunch: Farewell Meal
- Lunch Spot: Have a farewell meal at a local restaurant or café in St. Margaret's Hope or Kirkwall.

Afternoon: Final Exploration
- Highland Park Distiller: Tour the Highland Park Distillery and sample some of Orkney's finest whisky.

- Shopping: Do some last-minute shopping for Orkney crafts, produce, and souvenirs.

Late Afternoon: Departure
- Check-Out: Check out of your accommodation and head to the airport or ferry terminal.
- Travel Home: Depart from Orkney, taking with you memories of an unforgettable adventure.

Practical Tips
- Accommodation: Book in advance, especially during peak seasons. Consider staying in Kirkwall or Stromness for convenience.
- Transport: Renting a car is recommended for easy access to various sites. Alternatively, use local buses and ferries.
- Weather: Be prepared for changing weather. Pack layers, waterproof clothing, and sturdy footwear for outdoor activities.
- Local Etiquette: Respect local customs and natural sites. Leave no trace when exploring the outdoors.

This 5-day adventure itinerary offers a perfect mix of history, culture, and outdoor activities, allowing you to fully experience the magic of Orkney. From ancient Neolithic sites and stunning coastal cliffs to vibrant local culture and wildlife watching, you'll leave Orkney with lasting memories and a deep appreciation for this unique destination.

7-Day Immersive Experience

Orkney is a unique destination with a rich blend of history, culture, and natural beauty. This 7-day immersive itinerary will allow you to explore the islands thoroughly, providing a perfect balance of sightseeing, outdoor activities, and local experiences.

Day 1: Arrival and Initial Exploration
Morning: Arrival in Orkney
- Travel to Orkney: Arrive via flight to Kirkwall Airport or ferry to Stromness.
- Check-In: Settle into your accommodation in Kirkwall.

Late Morning: Discovering Kirkwall
- St. Magnus Cathedral: Begin with a visit to the iconic St. Magnus Cathedral, a magnificent example of medieval architecture.
- Orkney Museum: Learn about Orkney's rich history at the Orkney Museum, located nearby.

Lunch: Local Cuisine
- Lunch Spot: Enjoy a meal at a local café or restaurant such as The Reel or The Bothy.

Afternoon: Historical Sites

- Earl's Palace and Bishop's Palace: Explore the ruins of the Earl's Palace and the adjacent Bishop's Palace, both showcasing impressive Renaissance architecture.

Evening: Local Culture
- Dinner: Dine at a traditional restaurant like Helgi's or The Foveran.
- Local Pubs: Experience Orkney's nightlife at a local pub such as The Orkney Brewery or The Auld Motor Hoose.

Day 2: Neolithic Orkney and Coastal Exploration

Morning: Neolithic Heartland
- Skara Brae: Visit the well-preserved Neolithic village of Skara Brae and the nearby Skaill House.
- Ring of Brodgar: Explore the Ring of Brodgar, a dramatic stone circle.
- Standing Stones of Stenness: Visit the nearby Standing Stones of Stenness.

Lunch: Countryside Picnic
- Picnic: Enjoy a picnic lunch amidst the beautiful countryside or by the shore of a loch.

Afternoon: Coastal Beauty

- Yesnaby Cliffs: Walk along the stunning Yesnaby Cliffs, known for their dramatic sea stacks and Atlantic views.

Evening: Return to Kirkwall
- Dinner: Return to Kirkwall for dinner at a recommended restaurant.
- Relax: Relax and prepare for the next day's adventures.

Day 3: Island Hopping and Outdoor Adventures
Morning: Rousay Island
- Ferry to Rousay: Take a morning ferry to Rousay, known as the "Egypt of the North" for its archaeological sites.
- Taversoe Tuick and Midhowe Cairn: Visit these ancient burial sites and enjoy the island's natural beauty.

Lunch: Local Delights
- Rousay Lunch: Have lunch at a local café or enjoy a packed lunch by the coast.

Afternoon: Exploring Rousay
- Walks and Wildlife: Explore Rousay's walking trails and look out for local wildlife, including seals and seabirds.

Evening: Return to Mainland Orkney

- Ferry Back: Return to Mainland Orkney and have dinner in Kirkwall or Stromness.

Day 4: Outdoor Adventures and Scenic Drives
Morning: Brough of Birsay
- Visit Brough of Birsay: Cross the tidal causeway (check tide times) to explore the island's ruins and lighthouse.

Late Morning: Eynhallow Sound
- Wildlife Watching: Take a boat trip around Eynhallow Sound for excellent wildlife viewing, including puffins, seals, and possibly whales.

Lunch: Coastal Café
- Lunch Spot: Enjoy a meal at a coastal café such as the Birsay Bay Tearoom.

Afternoon: Scapa Flow
- Scapa Flow: Visit Scapa Flow Visitor Centre and Museum to learn about Orkney's wartime history.

Evening: Sunset at a Scenic Spot
- Dinner: Have dinner in Kirkwall or Stromness.
- Sunset Viewing: Watch the sunset from a scenic location such as Yesnaby Cliffs or Waulkmill Bay.

Day 5: South Ronaldsay and the Churchill Barriers

Morning: Italian Chapel and Churchill Barriers
- Italian Chapel: Visit the beautifully decorated Italian Chapel on Lamb Holm.
- Churchill Barriers: Drive across the Churchill Barriers and explore the scenic spots and wrecks.

Lunch: St. Margaret's Hope
- Lunch Spot: Enjoy a meal at a local restaurant or café in St. Margaret's Hope.

Afternoon: South Ronaldsay Sites
- Tomb of the Eagles: Visit the Tomb of the Eagles, a fascinating Neolithic chambered tomb with stunning coastal views.
- Walks and Wildlife: Explore the nature trails and watch for local wildlife.

Evening: Return to Kirkwall
- Dinner: Return to Kirkwall and dine at a local restaurant.
- Relax: Relax and enjoy the local ambiance.

Day 6: Hoy Island Exploration
Morning: Travel to Hoy
- Ferry to Hoy: Take the morning ferry to Hoy, the second-largest island in Orkney.

Late Morning: Rackwick Bay

- Rackwick Bay: Visit the beautiful Rackwick Bay, known for its dramatic cliffs and sandy beach.

Lunch: Picnic at Rackwick Bay
- Picnic: Enjoy a packed lunch at Rackwick Bay, taking in the stunning scenery.

Afternoon: Old Man of Hoy
- Old Man of Hoy: Hike to the Old Man of Hoy, a famous sea stack. The hike offers breathtaking views and a chance to experience Hoy's rugged landscape.

Evening: Return to Mainland Orkney
- Ferry Back: Return to Mainland Orkney and have dinner in Stromness or Kirkwall.

Day 7: Final Exploration and Departure
Morning: Stromness
- Explore Stromness: Wander the charming streets of Stromness, visit local shops, and enjoy the coastal views.
- Stromness Museum: Learn about the town's maritime history at the Stromness Museum.

Late Morning: Highland Park Distillery
- Highland Park Distillery: Tour the Highland Park Distillery and sample some of Orkney's finest whisky.

Lunch: Farewell Meal
- Lunch Spot: Have a farewell meal at a local restaurant or café in Kirkwall or Stromness.

Afternoon: Final Exploration
- Shopping: Do some last-minute shopping for Orkney crafts, produce, and souvenirs.

Late Afternoon: Departure
- Check-Out: Check out of your accommodation and head to the airport or ferry terminal.
- Travel Home: Depart from Orkney, taking with you memories of an unforgettable adventure.

Practical Tips
- Accommodation: Book in advance, especially during peak seasons. Consider staying in Kirkwall or Stromness for convenience.
- Transport: Renting a car is recommended for easy access to various sites. Alternatively, use local buses and ferries.
- Weather: Be prepared for changing weather. Pack layers, waterproof clothing, and sturdy footwear for outdoor activities.
- Local Etiquette: Respect local customs and natural sites. Leave no trace when exploring the outdoors.

This 7-day immersive itinerary offers a perfect mix of history, culture, and outdoor activities, allowing you to fully experience the magic of Orkney. From ancient Neolithic sites and stunning coastal cliffs to vibrant local culture and wildlife watching, you'll leave Orkney with lasting memories and a deep appreciation for this unique destination.

Chapter 10

ICONIC LANDMARKS AND TOP TOURISM SPOTS

Skara Brae

Skara Brae is one of Orkney's most iconic and fascinating landmarks. This remarkably well-preserved Neolithic village offers a unique glimpse into life over 5,000 years ago, making it an essential visit for history enthusiasts and casual travelers alike. Skara Brae is part of the Heart of Neolithic Orkney UNESCO World Heritage Site, which also includes Maeshowe, the Stones of Stenness, and the Ring of Brodgar.

Historical Significance
Discovery and Excavation

Skara Brae was uncovered by a storm in 1850, which exposed a cluster of stone buildings buried beneath the sand dunes. Subsequent excavations revealed a remarkably intact prehistoric village, providing invaluable insights into Neolithic life. The site consists of eight well-preserved stone houses connected by covered passageways, offering a snapshot of domestic life during the Neolithic period.

Daily Life in Skara Brae
The inhabitants of Skara Brae lived in small, close-knit communities. The houses were built with thick stone walls, and each house contained a central hearth, stone beds, and storage areas. The sophisticated construction included drainage systems and evidence of furniture carved from stone. Tools, pottery, and other artifacts found at the site indicate that the villagers were skilled craftsmen and traders.

Visiting Skara Brae

Getting There
Skara Brae is located on the west coast of Mainland Orkney, near the Bay of Skaill. It is easily accessible by car, with ample parking available at the site. Public transportation options include local buses from Kirkwall and Stromness.

Visitor Experience

- Visitor Centre: Begin your visit at the Skara Brae Visitor Centre, which provides an excellent introduction to the site. Interactive exhibits, informative displays, and a short film help to set the context for your exploration of the village.
- Reconstructed House: The visitor centre includes a full-scale replica of a Skara Brae house, allowing you to step back in time and experience what life was like for the Neolithic inhabitants. The replica showcases the interior layout, including the central hearth, stone furniture, and sleeping areas.
- Guided Tours: Guided tours are available and highly recommended. Knowledgeable guides provide detailed insights into the history and significance of Skara Brae, making the visit even more enriching.

Exploring the Site

The Village

Walking through the interconnected houses of Skara Brae, you'll be amazed at the level of preservation. The stone walls, passageways, and even the remnants of furniture are incredibly well-preserved. Information panels throughout the site provide details about the construction and use of each area.

The Bay of Skaill

The stunning Bay of Skaill forms a picturesque backdrop to Skara Brae. After exploring the village, take a stroll along the sandy beach and enjoy the beautiful coastal scenery. The bay is also a great spot for birdwatching and observing marine life.

Practical Information

Opening Hours and Admission

Skara Brae is open year-round, although hours may vary by season. Admission fees apply, and discounts are available for children, students, and seniors. It is advisable to check the official website for up-to-date information on opening times and ticket prices.

Facilities

The visitor centre includes a gift shop offering a range of souvenirs, books, and local crafts. There is also a café serving light refreshments, where you can relax and enjoy views of the bay.

A visit to Skara Brae is a journey back in time to the Neolithic era, offering a rare and fascinating glimpse into prehistoric life. The combination of well-preserved structures, informative exhibits, and the stunning natural setting makes Skara Brae a must-see landmark in Orkney. Whether you are a history buff, an archaeology enthusiast, or simply a curious traveler, Skara Brae is sure to leave a lasting impression.

Ring Of Brodgar

The Ring of Brodgar is one of Orkney's most iconic and awe-inspiring landmarks. This prehistoric stone circle is part of the Heart of Neolithic Orkney UNESCO World Heritage Site, which also includes Skara Brae, Maeshowe, and the Standing Stones of Stenness. The Ring of Brodgar is a must-visit for anyone interested in ancient history, archaeology, and the mystical allure of Neolithic monuments.

Historical Significance
Construction and Purpose
The Ring of Brodgar is believed to have been constructed between 2500 BC and 2000 BC, during the Neolithic period. It is a henge and stone circle comprising originally 60 stones, with 36 stones still

standing today. The exact purpose of the Ring of Brodgar remains a mystery, but it is thought to have been used for ceremonial or religious purposes, possibly related to astronomy and seasonal cycles.

Archaeological Findings
Archaeological excavations around the Ring of Brodgar have uncovered evidence of human activity dating back to the Neolithic period. These findings include pottery, tools, and animal bones, suggesting that the site was a focal point for gatherings and rituals. The sheer size and scale of the stone circle indicate its importance to the prehistoric communities that built it.

Visiting the Ring of Brodgar
Getting There
The Ring of Brodgar is located on the Mainland of Orkney, approximately 8 miles northwest of Kirkwall. It is easily accessible by car, with a designated parking area nearby. Public transportation options include local buses that stop near the site.

Visitor Experience
- Self-Guided Exploration: Visitors can freely explore the Ring of Brodgar at their own pace. The site is open year-round and offers a peaceful and contemplative atmosphere. Informative panels

around the site provide historical context and details about the stone circle's construction and significance.
- Guided Tours: For a more in-depth experience, consider joining a guided tour. Knowledgeable guides share fascinating insights into the history, archaeology, and legends associated with the Ring of Brodgar, enriching your understanding of this ancient monument.

Exploring the Site

The Stone Circle

Walking among the towering stones of the Ring of Brodgar is a humbling experience. The stone circle, which spans about 104 meters (341 feet) in diameter, is set within a natural amphitheater of hills and water, creating a dramatic and evocative landscape. The stones vary in height, with the tallest standing over 4.5 meters (15 feet) high.

The Surrounding Landscape

The Ring of Brodgar is situated in a stunning natural setting, surrounded by the Lochs of Harray and Stenness. The combination of the stone circle and the surrounding landscape creates a sense of timeless beauty and serenity. Visitors are encouraged to take a walk around the site to fully appreciate the interplay between the ancient stones and the natural environment.

Practical Information

Opening Hours and Admission

The Ring of Brodgar is open to the public year-round and admission is free. The site is maintained by Historic Environment Scotland, and donations are appreciated to help with the preservation of this important heritage site.

Facilities

There are no facilities directly at the Ring of Brodgar, but nearby attractions such as the Standing Stones of Stenness and Maeshowe offer visitor centers with restrooms, gift shops, and cafes. It is advisable to bring water and wear suitable clothing and footwear for walking, especially in wet or windy weather.

Nearby Attractions

Standing Stones of Stenness

Just a short distance from the Ring of Brodgar, the Standing Stones of Stenness are another significant Neolithic monument. This smaller stone circle dates back to around 3100 BC and is one of the earliest henge monuments in Britain.

Maeshowe

A few miles from the Ring of Brodgar, Maeshowe is a large chambered cairn and passage grave. It is renowned for its impressive construction and the runic inscriptions left by Viking visitors in the 12th century.

The Ring of Brodgar is a captivating and enigmatic landmark that offers a profound connection to Orkney's ancient past. Its sheer size, historical significance, and stunning natural setting make it a highlight of any visit to Orkney. Whether you are an avid history enthusiast, an archaeology buff, or simply someone who appreciates the beauty and mystery of ancient monuments, the Ring of Brodgar is sure to leave a lasting impression.

Maeshowe

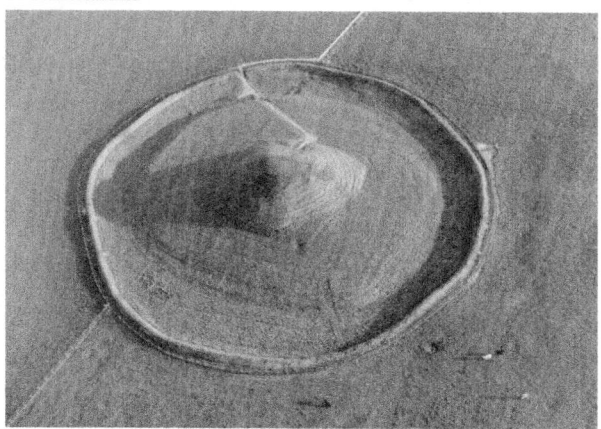

Maeshowe is one of the most iconic and significant prehistoric monuments in Orkney. This Neolithic chambered cairn and passage grave is a marvel of ancient engineering and craftsmanship, renowned for its impressive size, intricate construction, and fascinating history. As part of the Heart of Neolithic Orkney UNESCO World Heritage Site, Maeshowe offers visitors a unique window into the lives and beliefs of Orkney's early inhabitants.

Historical Significance

Construction and Purpose

Maeshowe was built around 2800 BC, during the late Neolithic period. The structure consists of a large, grass-covered mound, with an entrance passage leading to a central chamber surrounded by smaller cells. The precise construction of Maeshowe, with its carefully aligned stones and corbelled roof, indicates a high level of architectural skill. It is believed that Maeshowe served as a burial site and possibly a ceremonial center, reflecting the spiritual and communal practices of its builders.

Viking Inscriptions

In the 12th century, Maeshowe was entered by a group of Norsemen seeking shelter. These Viking visitors left behind a remarkable collection of runic inscriptions, making Maeshowe one of the largest and most important collections of runes in the British Isles. The inscriptions provide a fascinating glimpse into the lives and thoughts of these Norse visitors, adding an extra layer of historical intrigue to the site.

Visiting Maeshowe

Getting There
Maeshowe is located on Mainland Orkney, approximately 9 miles west of Kirkwall and 1.5 miles northeast of the Standing Stones of Stenness. The site is accessible by car, with parking available at the Maeshowe Visitor Centre. Public transportation options include local buses that stop nearby.

Visitor Experience
- Guided Tours: Access to Maeshowe is by guided tour only, ensuring that the site is protected and that visitors receive a comprehensive understanding of its significance. Knowledgeable guides provide detailed explanations of the site's history, construction, and the intriguing runic inscriptions left by the Vikings.
- Visitor Centre: Tours begin at the Maeshowe Visitor Centre in Stenness, where visitors can view exhibits and displays about the site's history and significance. The centre also has a gift shop offering souvenirs and books related to Orkney's archaeological heritage.

Exploring the Site

The Chambered Cairn
The entrance passage to Maeshowe is aligned to capture the setting sun at the winter solstice, illuminating the interior chamber in a spectacular display of light. This alignment suggests that Maeshowe had significant ceremonial or astronomical importance to its builders. Inside, the central chamber is constructed with precision-cut stones, creating a corbelled roof that has stood the test of time. The walls of the chamber and passage are adorned with the Viking runes, offering a unique blend of Neolithic and Norse heritage.

The Surrounding Landscape
Maeshowe is set within a landscape rich in archaeological sites, including the nearby Stones of Stenness, the Ring of Brodgar, and the Barnhouse Settlement. This concentration of ancient monuments within a relatively small area highlights the importance of this region in Neolithic Orkney. Visitors are encouraged to explore these nearby sites to gain a fuller understanding of the prehistoric landscape.

Practical Information

Opening Hours and Admission
Maeshowe is open to visitors year-round, though hours may vary by season. As guided tours are mandatory, it is advisable to book in advance,

especially during peak tourist seasons. Admission fees apply, with discounts available for children, students, and seniors. Check the official Historic Environment Scotland website for the most up-to-date information on opening times and ticket prices.

Facilities
The Maeshowe Visitor Centre provides restrooms and a gift shop. There are no facilities directly at the Maeshowe site itself, so it is recommended to visit the centre before or after your tour.

Nearby Attractions

Stones of Stenness
Located just a short distance from Maeshowe, the Stones of Stenness are part of the same UNESCO World Heritage Site. This stone circle, dating back to around 3100 BC, is one of the earliest henge monuments in Britain and provides further insight into Neolithic ceremonial practices.

Ring of Brodgar
Another nearby site, the Ring of Brodgar, is a dramatic stone circle and henge, offering stunning views and a sense of the monumental scale of Neolithic architecture in Orkney. It is believed to have been constructed around 2500 BC.

Maeshowe is a captivating and enigmatic landmark that offers a profound connection to Orkney's ancient past. Its remarkable construction, intriguing Viking inscriptions, and alignment with the winter solstice make it a site of both historical and archaeological importance. Whether you are a history enthusiast, an archaeology buff, or simply a curious traveler, a visit to Maeshowe will leave you with a deeper appreciation for the ingenuity and spirituality of Orkney's early inhabitants.

St. Magnus Cathedral

St Magnus Cathedral, often referred to as the "Light of the North," is one of Orkney's most iconic landmarks. Located in the heart of Kirkwall, the capital of Orkney, this magnificent structure stands as a testament to the islands' rich history and architectural prowess. Built in the 12th century, the cathedral is not only a place of worship but also a symbol of Orkney's Norse heritage and a must-visit destination for anyone exploring the islands.

Historical Significance

Construction and Origins

St Magnus Cathedral was founded in 1137 by the Viking Earl Rognvald to honor his uncle, St Magnus Erlendsson, who was martyred around 1117. The cathedral was built using red and yellow sandstone, giving it a distinctive and striking appearance. Its construction spanned several centuries, resulting in a blend of Romanesque and Gothic architectural styles.

St Magnus and His Legacy

St Magnus was canonized as a saint, and his remains were interred in the cathedral, which became a site of pilgrimage. The stories of his piety and martyrdom are central to Orkney's history and identity. The cathedral stands as a lasting tribute to his legacy and the Christianization of the Norse inhabitants of Orkney.

Architectural Highlights

Exterior Features

The exterior of St Magnus Cathedral is characterized by its tall, imposing structure and the use of red and yellow sandstone. The intricate carvings and the beautiful west front are notable features. The central tower, rising above the town of Kirkwall, is a prominent feature of the Orkney skyline.

Interior Beauty
The interior of the cathedral is equally impressive, with a long nave flanked by massive pillars and arches. The combination of Romanesque solidity and Gothic elegance creates a space that is both awe-inspiring and serene. Notable features include the stained glass windows, the magnificent vaulted ceiling, and the elaborate carvings on the choir stalls and pulpit.

Visiting St Magnus Cathedral
Getting There
St Magnus Cathedral is located in the center of Kirkwall, making it easily accessible on foot from most parts of the town. If you are arriving by car, there are several parking options nearby. Kirkwall is also well-connected by bus services, with stops close to the cathedral.

Visitor Experience
- Self-Guided Tours: Visitors can explore the cathedral at their own pace. Informational plaques and leaflets available at the entrance provide

historical context and details about the cathedral's features.

- Guided Tours: For a more in-depth experience, consider joining a guided tour. Knowledgeable guides share fascinating stories about the cathedral's history, architecture, and the legends of St Magnus.

- Opening Hours and Admission: The cathedral is generally open to visitors year-round, though hours may vary, especially during special services or events. Admission is free, but donations are welcome to help with the maintenance of this historic site.

Key Attractions

The Tomb of St Magnus

One of the highlights of visiting St Magnus Cathedral is the opportunity to see the tomb of St Magnus. Located in the choir, this simple yet poignant memorial marks the final resting place of Orkney's patron saint.

The Rose Window

The stunning rose window in the east end of the cathedral is a masterpiece of stained glass art. It depicts scenes from the life of St Magnus and adds to the spiritual and aesthetic appeal of the cathedral.

The Orkneyinga Saga

The Orkneyinga Saga, a historical narrative of the Norse earls of Orkney, features prominently in the cathedral's history. Visitors can learn about the saga and its significance through displays and interpretive materials within the cathedral.

Memorials and Monuments
Throughout the cathedral, there are numerous memorials and monuments dedicated to notable figures from Orkney's history. These include gravestones, plaques, and effigies, each with its own story to tell.

Practical Information

Facilities
The cathedral has basic visitor facilities, including restrooms and a small gift shop where you can purchase souvenirs, books, and local crafts. There are also several cafes and restaurants nearby where you can enjoy refreshments before or after your visit.

Accessibility
St Magnus Cathedral is accessible to visitors with mobility issues, with ramps and assistance available for those who need it. However, some areas of the cathedral, such as the upper galleries, may have limited access.

Nearby Attractions

<u>The Earl's Palace and Bishop's Palace</u>

Just a short walk from the cathedral, these two historic palaces offer further insights into Orkney's rich past. The Earl's Palace, built in the early 17th century, is a fine example of Renaissance architecture, while the Bishop's Palace dates back to the 12th century and offers stunning views over Kirkwall.

<u>Orkney Museum</u>

Located in Tankerness House, close to the cathedral, the Orkney Museum provides a comprehensive overview of Orkney's history, from the Neolithic period to the present day. It's a great place to learn more about the context in which St Magnus Cathedral was built and its significance over the centuries.

St Magnus Cathedral is a jewel in Orkney's crown, offering visitors a unique combination of historical, architectural, and spiritual experiences. Whether you are drawn by its stunning architecture, its deep historical roots, or the legends of St Magnus, a visit to this magnificent cathedral is sure to be a highlight of your trip to Orkney. As you explore its hallowed halls and take in its serene beauty, you'll gain a deeper appreciation for the rich cultural heritage of the Orkney Islands.

The Old Man Of Hoy

The Old Man of Hoy, located on the island of Hoy in Orkney, Scotland, is a striking sea stack that stands as a natural wonder and a magnet for adventurers and nature lovers. Here's a comprehensive look at why it captivates visitors:

Geological Marvel:
The Old Man of Hoy is a towering sea stack, rising 137 meters (450 feet) above the restless waters of the North Sea. Formed from red sandstone, it stands as a testament to the erosive forces of wind and water over millennia, creating a dramatic and awe-inspiring sight against the Orkney coastline.

Climbing Challenge:

For climbers and mountaineers, the Old Man of Hoy presents a formidable challenge. Its sheer vertical sides and exposed location make it a renowned climb in the world of rock climbing. Adventurers from around the globe are drawn to conquer its cliffs, experiencing both the physical demands and the exhilaration of scaling such an iconic natural formation.

Natural Habitat:
The area around the Old Man of Hoy is also rich in wildlife, offering opportunities for birdwatching and nature photography. The sea cliffs provide nesting sites for various seabirds, including puffins, razorbills, and guillemots, making it a paradise for bird enthusiasts during the breeding season.

Access and Facilities:
Access to the Old Man of Hoy typically involves a short ferry ride from mainland Orkney to Hoy, followed by a hike along scenic coastal paths to reach the viewing points overlooking the sea stack. Visitors can enjoy facilities such as visitor centers, guided tours, and accommodation options ranging from campsites to cozy guesthouses.

Cultural and Historical Context:
Hoy itself is steeped in history, with ancient archaeological sites and reminders of Orkney's

Viking past nearby. The landscape around the Old Man of Hoy offers a blend of natural beauty and cultural heritage, making it an enriching destination for those interested in history and archaeology.

The Old Man of Hoy stands as a symbol of Orkney's rugged natural beauty and offers visitors a chance to engage with its geological wonders, wildlife, and adventurous spirit. Whether you come to climb its cliffs, observe seabirds, or simply marvel at its grandeur, a visit to the Old Man of Hoy promises an unforgettable experience amidst Scotland's northern isles.

Scapa Flow

Scapa Flow, situated in Orkney, Scotland, is a renowned destination for both history enthusiasts and divers alike. Here's a detailed overview of why it attracts visitors:

Historical Significance:
Scapa Flow holds immense historical importance, notably serving as the main British naval base during both World War I and World War II. It was the site of the German High Seas Fleet's scuttling in 1919, a dramatic event where 74 ships were deliberately sunk by their crews to prevent them from falling into enemy hands. This event is still remembered and explored by historians and visitors.

Diving Attractions:
The sunken remnants of the German fleet make Scapa Flow a paradise for wreck divers. These well-preserved wrecks lie at various depths, offering divers a unique opportunity to explore history underwater. The wrecks are often covered in marine life, creating a captivating underwater ecosystem.

Natural Beauty:
Beyond its historical significance, Scapa Flow boasts stunning natural beauty. The clear waters and picturesque coastline of Orkney provide a serene backdrop for various outdoor activities, from sailing to wildlife watching.

Cultural and Heritage Sites:

Orkney itself is rich in Neolithic and Viking heritage, with sites like Skara Brae, a UNESCO World Heritage Site, offering insights into ancient civilizations. Visitors to Scapa Flow often combine their explorations with visits to these archaeological wonders.

Practical Information:
Visitors can access Scapa Flow via ferries from mainland Scotland or flights to Orkney's Kirkwall Airport. Accommodation options range from cozy B&Bs to hotels, catering to different preferences and budgets.

Scapa Flow's allure lies in its blend of historical intrigue, natural beauty, and vibrant marine life. Whether you're a history buff eager to explore wartime relics or a diver seeking adventure beneath the waves, Scapa Flow promises a memorable experience that blends history, nature, and culture in a unique Scottish setting.

Brough Of Birsay

The Brough of Birsay, located on the northwestern coast of Mainland Orkney, Scotland, is a captivating historical and natural site that attracts visitors from around the world. Here's a comprehensive overview of why it is considered a top tourist destination:

Historical Significance:
The Brough of Birsay holds significant historical importance dating back to the Viking Age and earlier. It was once a Pictish and later a Norse settlement, serving as a seat of power for Viking chieftains. The remains of Norse buildings, including a church and a monastery, provide glimpses into its rich past, making it a fascinating site for history enthusiasts.

Dramatic Coastal Setting:

Perched on a tidal island, the Brough of Birsay is accessible on foot only during low tide via a causeway, adding an element of adventure to the visitor experience. The rugged coastal scenery surrounding the island, with its cliffs and panoramic views of the Atlantic Ocean, enhances its allure as a natural and historical site.

Archaeological Discoveries:
Excavations on the Brough have unearthed artifacts ranging from Pictish symbols to Norse artifacts, offering insights into the island's diverse cultural history. Archaeological remains, including a Norse settlement and the remnants of an early Christian church, provide tangible connections to Orkney's ancient past.

Wildlife and Nature:
The Brough of Birsay is also a haven for birdwatchers, particularly during the breeding season when seabirds such as puffins and fulmars nest along the cliffs. The coastal habitats around the island support a variety of flora and fauna, adding to its ecological appeal.

Visitor Facilities:
Visitors to the Brough of Birsay can explore the island's archaeological sites and natural beauty at their own pace, with interpretive signage providing

historical context. Facilities such as parking areas, visitor centers, and guided tours are available to enhance the visitor experience and understanding of the site's significance.

Practical Information:
Access to the Brough of Birsay involves checking tidal timetables to plan visits safely during low tide. Ferries from mainland Orkney and nearby islands provide transportation to Mainland, where visitors can drive or take public transport to the Brough.

The Brough of Birsay stands as a testament to Orkney's rich cultural heritage and natural beauty, offering visitors a unique opportunity to explore ancient ruins, experience dramatic coastal landscapes, and witness diverse wildlife in a historically significant setting. Whether you come for its historical intrigue, natural wonders, or a combination of both, a visit to the Brough of Birsay promises a memorable journey through Scotland's northern isles.

Italian Chapel

The Italian Chapel, located on the island of Lamb Holm in Orkney, Scotland, is a remarkable testament to human creativity, resilience, and artistic expression. Here's a comprehensive overview of why it is considered a top tourist destination:

Historical Context:
During World War II, Italian prisoners of war (POWs) were interned in Orkney and tasked with constructing the Churchill Barriers, causeways designed to protect the Royal Navy's fleet in Scapa Flow. Among these prisoners were skilled craftsmen who transformed two Nissen huts into a chapel, demonstrating incredible ingenuity and dedication amidst the harsh conditions of war.

Architectural Beauty:
The Italian Chapel is renowned for its exquisite interior, adorned with intricate frescoes and decorative details hand-painted by the POWs. The chapel's facade features a stunning facade resembling a Romanesque church, complete with a bell tower and ornate ironwork, crafted from salvaged materials and surplus concrete.

Symbol of Peace and Reconciliation:
Beyond its architectural significance, the Italian Chapel serves as a poignant symbol of peace and reconciliation between former adversaries. It stands as a testament to the human spirit's ability to find beauty and solace even in the darkest times, transcending nationalities and conflicts.

Visitor Experience:
Visitors to the Italian Chapel can explore its interior, marveling at the craftsmanship of the POWs and reflecting on its historical significance. Guided tours and interpretive displays provide insights into the chapel's construction and the lives of the prisoners who created it, offering a deeper understanding of its cultural and historical importance.

Cultural Heritage:

The Italian Chapel has been meticulously preserved over the decades, maintaining its original charm and historical integrity. It remains a place of worship and pilgrimage for both locals and visitors, highlighting its enduring cultural relevance and impact on Orkney's heritage.

Practical Information:
Access to the Italian Chapel is straightforward, with ferries connecting Orkney's mainland to Lamb Holm. Visitor facilities, including parking, interpretive exhibits, and gift shops, enhance the experience of exploring this iconic site.

The Italian Chapel stands as a remarkable example of human resilience and artistic achievement, attracting visitors from around the world who come to admire its beauty, reflect on its history, and appreciate its role in promoting peace and understanding. A visit to the Italian Chapel offers a profound journey through wartime history and the enduring power of hope and creativity.

CONCLUSION

Final Tips And Recommendations

1. Plan Ahead for Ferry Services: Orkney's islands are well-connected by regular ferry services, but schedules can vary with the seasons. It's advisable to check and book ferry tickets in advance, especially during peak tourist times, to ensure smooth transportation between islands and mainland Orkney.

2. Respect Nature and Wildlife: Orkney's landscapes are pristine and home to diverse wildlife, including seabird colonies and marine life. Respect local wildlife habitats by following designated paths, avoiding disturbing nesting birds, and adhering to any conservation guidelines in place.

3. Check Tidal Timetables: When visiting tidal islands like the Brough of Birsay, the tidal causeway to the island is only accessible during low tide. Plan your visit according to tidal timetables available locally or online to avoid being stranded or missing out on exploring these unique sites.

4. Embrace Orkney's Culinary Delights: Orkney is renowned for its local produce and seafood. Sample traditional Orcadian dishes like Orkney beef, fresh seafood (including renowned Orkney scallops), and artisanal cheeses. Visit local farmers' markets or restaurants to savor the flavors of the islands.

5. Explore Beyond the Main Sites: While Orkney's main attractions like Skara Brae and the Ring of Brodgar are must-sees, don't miss out on exploring lesser-known gems. Discover charming villages, coastal walks, and hidden archaeological sites that showcase Orkney's rich history and natural beauty away from the crowds.

6. Weather Preparedness: Orkney's weather can be unpredictable, with brisk winds and occasional rain even in summer. Pack layers, waterproof clothing, and sturdy footwear suitable for outdoor activities. Be prepared for changing weather conditions to fully enjoy your explorations.

7. Engage with Local Culture: Orkney has a vibrant cultural scene with art galleries, craft workshops, and music festivals celebrating local traditions. Take time to engage with Orcadian culture through visiting local museums, attending traditional music events, or participating in guided tours that highlight the island's heritage.

8. Support Sustainable Tourism: Contribute to sustainable tourism practices by supporting local businesses, respecting cultural heritage sites, and minimizing your environmental impact. Choose eco-friendly accommodations and transportation options where possible to help preserve Orkney's natural beauty for future generations.

9. Capture Memories Responsibly: Orkney's landscapes and historic sites offer countless opportunities for photography. Be mindful of local regulations regarding photography in sensitive areas, such as archaeological sites, and ask for permission when photographing private property or local residents.

10. Enjoy the Journey: Above all, embrace the tranquility and unique charm of Orkney. Whether you're exploring ancient ruins, admiring coastal vistas, or simply soaking in the peaceful

atmosphere, allow yourself to immerse in the island's beauty and history at your own pace.

Staying Connected With Orkney

Staying connected while visiting Orkney ensures that visitors can easily navigate the islands, stay in touch with loved ones, and access essential information. Here are several ways visitors can stay connected:

1. Mobile Networks: Orkney has good mobile network coverage, especially in populated areas and main towns like Kirkwall and Stromness. Major UK mobile operators such as EE, Vodafone, O2, and Three provide coverage across the islands. However, coverage may vary in more remote or rural areas.

2. Internet Access:
 - Wi-Fi: Many accommodations, cafes, restaurants, and visitor centers in Orkney offer free Wi-Fi for guests. It's common to find Wi-Fi hotspots in tourist hubs like Kirkwall and Stromness.
 - Hotels and Guesthouses: Most hotels, guesthouses, and B&Bs in Orkney provide complimentary Wi-Fi access to their guests.

- Public Wi-Fi: Some public spaces, such as libraries and community centers, may offer free or low-cost Wi-Fi access. Check locally for availability and access instructions.

3. SIM Cards and Mobile Data:
   - Visitors can purchase local SIM cards from mobile network providers in Orkney. This option is ideal for those who need continuous mobile data access for navigation, communication, and social media.
   - Mobile data plans in Orkney typically offer 4G coverage, ensuring fast and reliable internet access across most parts of the islands.

4. Visitor Information Centers:
   - Orkney's Visitor Information Centers, located in main towns like Kirkwall and Stromness, provide access to maps, brochures, and helpful advice for tourists. They may also offer Wi-Fi access and internet terminals for visitors to use.

5. Travel Apps and Websites:
   - Utilize travel apps and websites to plan your journey, access real-time information on ferry schedules, local attractions, and events happening in Orkney. Many apps work offline once downloaded, which is useful for navigating areas with limited internet connectivity.

6. Emergency Services and Contacts:
   - Save emergency contact numbers, including local police, medical services, and accommodation providers, in your phone for quick access in case of emergencies or unexpected situations.

7. Postal Services:
   - Orkney has reliable postal services for sending postcards, letters, and packages. Post offices in major towns like Kirkwall and Stromness offer postal and courier services, along with additional amenities like currency exchange and banking services.

8. Digital Detox Options:
   - For those seeking a break from constant connectivity, Orkney's serene landscapes and peaceful atmosphere offer opportunities to unplug and enjoy nature without distractions. Embrace the tranquility and scenic beauty of the islands while disconnecting from digital devices.

By leveraging these connectivity options, visitors to Orkney can stay informed, connected, and make the most of their exploration of this captivating archipelago in Scotland.

Made in United States
North Haven, CT
05 June 2025

69515851R00143